NAKED SCOTLAND

An American Insider Bares All

Written, Illustrated, & Photographed by
S. Blyth Stirling

*Dedicated to my dad, GRW — lover of Laphroaig,
who sadly never made it to Dunnottar Castle.*

TABLE OF CONTENTS

introduction

This was me, age 20, a fresh-faced American in Scotland.

WHEN I was a few months shy of 20, I did something virtually unheard of back in those days — I met my boyfriend on the internet. And, he was Scottish. We found each other completely by accident in a primitive chat room, back in the dark ages before social media. We were both artistic types with the same ridiculous sense of humor, so we had an instant connection, and we got on like a house on fire. Even though we'd never met, somehow we never seemed to run out of things to talk about, and I plowed through the minutes of countless cheap international phone cards so we could speak nearly every day. (Skype wasn't a thing yet.)

Later that year, when we finally met in person over my Christmas break, we knew 3,000 miles was too much space between us. But, as a sophomore in college, I knew the only way we could be together was for me to study abroad, which meant moving from Boston, Massachusetts to Glasgow, Scotland.

Like a typical American with "Scottish roots", Scotland had always had this strange magnetic pull on me from a very early age, even though I'd never been there. Needless to say, the decision to take this enormous leap of faith was an easy one for me. When I eventually got accepted at a university in Glasgow and had my student visa in hand, I was beyond thrilled. (You could clearly see my excitement in my passport photo taken back then. In those days, smiles were still allowed.) I was ready for anything this whirlwind adventure would throw at me. Tartan, bagpipes, accents… bring it on.

Well, the day I actually moved into my boyfriend's house in a small village outside of Glasgow, armed with nothing more than jetlag and an overstuffed suitcase with "Heavy" tags flapping in the wind, nothing could have prepared me for just how *unprepared* I actually was. Despite moving many times growing up, I soon knew I was clearly in over my head. I had to relearn *everything*, even a new language. Friendly people were all around me, and yet I couldn't even understand what they were saying! Cultural references eluded me. Nothing made sense anymore.

Though I was grateful to have a Scottish boyfriend around for company, I soon found myself increasingly dependent on him as both my navigator and interpreter everywhere we went. Instead of feeling like a free spirit on a wild adventure, I started to feel more and more like I was living up to that "dumb blonde" stereotype, helplessly and hopelessly confused. That was not who I was at all, so I grew very self-conscious. At one point I remember being hesitant to even open my mouth in public to avoid drawing attention to my American-ness. I was tired of feeling like an outsider looking in.

I could have really used an insider's guide, written from an American perspective. Maybe then I could have understood exactly *what* I was getting myself into first.

That's why I wrote this book.

Granted, there were (and are) already *plenty* of books out there highlighting the differences between the UK and the US, which I had studied word for word. You know, "two nations divided by a common language" and all of that. However, I noticed all of these books are written with *England* in the spotlight. That's fine for Anglophiles, but not much use to someone who wants to know more about Scotland and all things Scottish.

See, England and Scotland might be on the same little island, and they share much of the same common culture. But once you scratch the surface, they are two very different countries, and they differ in more ways than you might expect. (First tip of this book: never imply Scotland is not a "real" country, even jokingly. Let's just say it will *not* be taken lightly!)

If you're reading this, you're probably in a similar situation as I was: maybe you're an American in a relationship with a Scot and want to understand them a bit better. Or maybe you're about to move over there, for school or work. Or perhaps you're about to visit Scotland as a tourist, and want to know a bit more than touristy travel guides and slang dictionaries let on. Whatever your reason, this book was written with you in mind, and I sincerely hope it helps even just a little bit.

I tried to cover a wide range of what you'll probably encounter in everyday life as an American in Scotland, and what it all means. (If you're *not* an American, I appreciate your interest and hope you can get something out of this book too.)

What this book is *not*, is a travel guide. There are plenty of travel guides on Scotland out there too, telling you what to see and do, and when to do them. It also doesn't go into how to move to Scotland, or the practical legal matters of living or working in Scotland. It's more of a cultural guide, based on what I've picked up via observation/osmosis over the years — everything you won't find anywhere else all in one place.

That Scottish boyfriend who stood beside me in my earliest days is now my husband, and somehow we've already been together for 15 years now. Although we have been living in America together now for over a decade (after my three-year student visa expired), Scotland remains a huge part of my life. We go back to visit as often as we can with our two young kids. His family is my family, and Scotland is home to me.

If you've actually bothered reading all of this, you might be wondering *why* I'm writing a book about Scotland when I'm now living in America, 3,000 miles away. Well, the way I see it, if I were writing this while living in Scotland, I wouldn't have the perspective as an outside observer anymore. I'd overlook the differences that you'd probably be most interested in reading about, because they would be a mundane part of my everyday life. Like an oversized impressionist painting, *sometimes things come into focus only when you step back from them.*

disclaimer

This book is based upon my personal, authentic experiences and observations as an American from Boston who has been part of a Scottish family for 15 years. It was written from my own personal demographic standpoint. Obviously, my experience will never perfectly match someone else's. I fully acknowledge that.

I lived and studied in Scotland's largest and most populated city, Glasgow, so you'll find my experiences tend to be Glasgow-centric. This book might be slightly different if I lived in posh Edinburgh or the rural Highlands, for example. (Sadly, I'm only one person, and I can't have the experience of living everywhere.) Also, because Scotland shares the same little island with England and Wales, many things I mention are true of, but might not be entirely unique to Scotland. But let's be honest: if I included annoying disclaimers like this on every little point, this book would get twice as long and twice as boring pretty fast.

My only hope is that you sit back, relax and enjoy reading this book as much as I've enjoyed writing it, and that you'll at least gain some deeper understanding of a culture and a country I know well, and love very much.

1

the ABCs of scotland:
a wee overview

YOU WOULDN'T hop into the driver's seat of a brand new car and expect to enjoy your time the behind the wheel if you didn't know how to drive. The same logic applies when you visit a new country. If you want to get the most out of your time there, a little background (beyond what the tourist industry tells you) is key. Let's begin with the absolute basics, in alphabetical order. (An added bonus: you're sure to impress the Scots you meet if you're already familiar with these things.)

A is for ALBA

Alba is the Scottish Gaelic name for Scotland. It's pronounced Al-a-pah. There's a channel on TV called BBC Alba which broadcasts entirely in Scottish Gaelic.

B is for BAGPIPES

The Great Highland Bagpipes, or "the pipes" for short, are well-known for being Scotland's national instrument. You'll mostly hear them played in heavily trafficked tourist areas nowadays, but their original purpose was to intimidate enemies on the battlefield.

C is for CALEDONIA

Caledonia is the poetic name for Scotland, particularly the Highlands. It's actually the Roman name for Northern Britain. There's a university in Glasgow called Glasgow Caledonian.

D is for DIALECT

Obviously, most people know that Scottish people speak English. So, just English with a Scottish accent, right? Um... nope. (I found this one out pretty quickly. I could barely understand what anyone was saying for a lot longer than I'd like to admit.)

Scottish people speak *Scots*, a dialect that developed in parallel with English for centuries. After Scotland and England united, however, upper class Scots began trying to distance themselves from their language, seeing it as an embarrassment. Schools played a large part in enforcing this attitude via corporal punishment, meaning shame about the way they talked was literally beaten into kids from an early age. Because of this, many unique Scots words have been lost forever.

Although attitudes have changed dramatically, even today, many speakers will code-switch to Scottish Standard English (a mixture of British English with some Scots) in formal situations, or with non-Scots. Even though Scottish people today are fiercely proud of their unique language, Scottish Standard English is still seen as the so-called "polite" way of talking.

The fusion of Scots and English means that if you're at all familiar with British English, you'll be well on your way to understanding the Scots. (*Lift* = elevator, *chips* = French fries, etc.) After all, most of the media in Scotland is filtered in from England. Even so, many words and phrases from England are *not* used in Scotland at all. (You won't hear Scottish people saying *"cor blimey!"* for example.)

E is for ENGLAND

If Scotland and England were on social media, their relationship status would be "It's Complicated". (They're almost always on the verge of breaking up too.) But contrary to popular belief, most Scots don't actually *hate* the English. However, pretending to hate them is still somewhat of a national pastime. (Hey, it goes both ways.) For example, Scots will involuntarily cheer for whatever sports team is playing against their "Auld Enemy". It's practically in their DNA.

It's true, however, that England does tend to bask in the world spotlight, leaving Scotland, Wales and Northern Ireland in its shadow. When most people hear "United Kingdom", they really hear *England.* (Or worse, jolly old London.) And when they say "British", they really mean *English.* (Even though Scotland is a country  in Great Britain, and therefore Scottish people are British too. Although many would never call themselves such. Scottish first, always.)

It's easy to see why the rest of the UK feels like an afterthought on the world map.

Here's how things typically play out: whenever a champion Scottish athlete loses, they are reported as Scottish by the dominant English media. But when they win, they're reported as *British*. And people around the world think British = English. You see? Scots just can't win.

And lastly, here is a typical conversation every Scot has experienced at least once in their lifetime:

Non-Scottish Person: I love your accent! Where are you from?
Scottish Person: Scotland.
Non-Scottish Person: Oohh, what part of England is that?!
Scottish Person: *facepalm*

F is for FLOWER OF SCOTLAND
Flower of Scotland is the unofficial National Anthem. You're most likely to hear it sung at sporting events which bring out Scottish pride. A perfect example of this would be a boxing match, when there's a Scottish boxer fighting another nationality. You'd think the song has deep historical roots, but it was actually written in the late 1960s by The Corries, a Scottish folk group.

The official flower of Scotland, if you were wondering, is the thistle. (In England, it's the rose and Wales the daffodil.) If you pay attention, you'll start to notice that thistles are just about everywhere, from motorway signage to company logos to the official Scotland police badge. Many places have Thistle in the name too. There's also a football (soccer) team called Partick Thistle.

G is for GAELIC

Scottish Gaelic (pronounced gal-lick, not gay-lick) is the Celtic (pronounced kel-tik) language spoken in the Highlands until the mid 1700s. Hardly anyone speaks it now (less than 1% of the population and shrinking). But Scotland stays true to its roots — bilingual English-Gaelic signs are everywhere, and the further north you go, the more you'll see. And at almost every train stop the place name will have its Gaelic name below.

H is for HAGGIS

Scotland's most infamous dish by far is haggis (pronounced HAG-gis), a mix of offal (animal organs) and oatmeal stuffed in a sheep's stomach. For all its notoriety, it still makes a regular appearance in everyday cuisine. Toasties, breakfast, pizzas, pakora...you name it, they *will* put haggis in it. And canned haggis is also a thing... if you dare. (I don't.) Thankfully for the less adventurous, there are vegetarian versions available. As for the origins of haggis, it was created as a way to avoid wasting oatmeal and offal, both of which were very hard to preserve otherwise. Waste not, want not, I suppose?

I is for INVENTIONS

We can thank Scottish inventors for a disproportionate number of inventions that we take for granted today, including (but not limited to) the flush toilet, the TV, the ATM, the microwave, refrigeration, waterproof paint, the raincoat, penicillin, and gin & tonic. (I'll drink to that!)

J is for JOCK

Jock is a mild slur for a Scottish person. Others include Big Mac and Caber Tosser. (Scotophobia is a real word, but it unfortunately doesn't mean what you think it means though. It means fear of the dark.)

K is for KILTS

It's actually true, Scottish men really do wear kilts. But the majority of men will only ever wear them at weddings in their lifetimes, and they're usually just rented. (So you won't find a kilt dangling in every Scotsman's wardrobe, sorry.) If you're lucky enough to be marrying a Scot, I'd say a wedding with kilts is definitely one of the perks. You will occasionally see kilted men moseying down the street. And sometimes kilts are worn (with T-shirts) at sporting events or music festivals. That's a thing too. Just a hint: never call it a skirt, even jokingly. It won't go down very well. (But *you* probably will.) As for what's under that kilt? Well…

L is for LOWLANDS AND HIGHLANDS

Scotland is divided into two unofficial regions: The Lowlands and the Highlands. The Highlands are anywhere north of the Highland Boundary Fault (including the northern Islands), and the Lowlands are anywhere south and east of it (including the Borders). The majority of Scots live in the Lowlands, where all the major cities (and therefore jobs) are, but the Highlands are where you'll find the highest concentration of striking natural beauty that Scotland is famous for.

Lowlanders call Highlanders "Teuchters", implying they're Gaelic-speaking country bumpkins. And Highlanders call Lowlanders "Sassenachs" (Saxons), implying they're more English than Scottish. Both are mock insults that aren't usually taken very seriously anymore.

M is for MC- AND MAC-

There's a myth that a surname that starts with Mc- is Irish, and Mac- is Scottish. But in reality, it's the exact same word, just spelled differently. Both come from the same old Gaelic word *meic*, meaning "Son of", so both can be either Scottish or Irish. (Surnames with O', on the other hand, are always Irish.)

N is for NAMES

Here are a few first names you'll encounter on a regular basis in Scotland that you might not hear very often anywhere else:

Men: Alasdair, Hamish, Lewis, Callum, Duncan, Fraser, Angus, Arran, Ewan (or Euan), Graeme, Gregor, Jock, Magnus, Rab, Tam (nickname for Thomas), Shug (nickname for Hugh), Rory

Women: Morag, Mags, Eilidh/Ailidh (pronounced Ay-lee), Elspeth, Iona, Isla (pronounced Eye-la), Kirsty, Rhona, Niamh (pronounced Neev)

O is for OLD FIRM

Celtic and Rangers, Glasgow's two main football (soccer) teams, are known collectively as "The Old Firm". The rivalry between the two teams is very deeply embedded in Scottish culture. (And it goes way deeper than just football for the fans, as you'll read about later on.)

By the way, just so you don't embarrass yourself: Celtic is pronounced SELL-tick (but it's never The Celtics, even though Boston's basketball team is also pronounced with the soft C, weirdly). And Rangers is never *The* Rangers. So it's Celtic and Rangers. That's it.

P is for PLAID

What we Americans think of as plaid (that criss-cross pattern on kilts) is called tartan in Scotland. In Scotland, a plaid is something else entirely: a piece of fabric draped across the chest when wearing a kilt. Originally, tartan was only really worn in the Highlands, but then the English banned it in the 1700s in an attempt to control warrior clans. When the ban was lifted, Scots rebelled by adopting it as their national costume. However, with the exception of kilts, the only people who wear tartan in Scotland today are tourists. In fact, that's a surefire way to spot one.

Q is for QUIRKY PRONUNCIATIONS

You'll run into many Scottish place names that'll trip you up, but the most commonly mispronounced are actually both of Scotland's major cities. Edinburgh is EM-bra (never Ed-in-burg), and Glasgow is GLAZ-goh (never Glass-cow). Loch is loCCHHH, not "lock" (with that throat-clearing/

cat-hissing sound.) Loch Lomond is Pronounced
LOH-mund, not luh-MOND.

Other classic trip-ups:

Milngavie	mull-GUY
Kircudbright	kir-KOO-bray
Anstruther	AIN-ster
Oban	OH-bin
Strathaven	STRAY-vin
Wemyss	weems
Garioch	GEE-ree
Islay	EYE-lah
Culzean (Castle)	kul-LEEN

R is for RED HAIR

In Scotland-themed tourist shops, they usually sell a
gag gift called a "See You Jimmy" hat, which is a tartan
bonnet with fake orange hair sticking out from under it.
Because *all* Scottish people have red hair, right? Actually,
that's not too far from the truth, because about 35% of Scots
carry the ginger gene in their DNA, second in the world only
to Ireland.

But if you walk down city streets expecting a sea of
carrot tops, you'll be disappointed. In fact, you probably
won't see any at all. This is because having red hair is seen

as an unforgivable flaw and everyone from school children to full-grown adults will torment you for it. The hatred of this basic human hair pigmentation verges on ridiculous, but it's inescapable. Therefore, most would-be gingers dye their hair. It's true that there are a lot of redheads — they're just in "stealth mode".

Sidenote: Ginger means redhead, but in Glasgow it is *also* the word used for any carbonated soft drink.

S is for SCOTCH

Scotch may be the American word for whisky, but don't use it for anything else. Scots or Scottish is correct. You'll still see the word occasionally (Scotch eggs, Scotch broth) but other than that, most Scots today find it vaguely condescending.

T is for TARTANRY

Tartanry is the overuse of tartan and kitschy Scottish imagery to portray an oversimplified and overly sentimental view of Scotland and its history. It was originally created by the Scottish tourism industry, and then further distorted by the American media. If you think everyone in Scotland is a kilt-wearing, bagpipe-playing, haggis-munching Highlander, that's tartanry at work.

U is for UNICORN

Scotland's national animal is the unicorn. (How awesome is that?!) The Scottish unicorn and the English lion face off with each other on the UK's Royal Coat of Arms. (It's no accident that the lion and the unicorn are sworn enemies in mythology!)

V is for VIKING TIES

Thanks to Viking invasions and proximity to Scandinavia, Nordic influences are still felt to this day in Scotland. Way up north on the Shetland islands, they even hold an annual yuletide Viking fire festival called Up Helly Aa. Many words we think of as 100% Scottish are actually Nordic (and have equivalents in Norwegian, Danish and Swedish).

Scottish	Viking
Greet (cry)	Græd
Een (eyes)	Øjne
Keek (look)	Kigge
Bairn (child)	Barn
Reek (smoke)	Røg
Muckle (much)	Meget
Kilt	Kjalta
Hame (home)	Hjem
Braw (good)	Bra
Ken (know)	Kende
Flit (move house)	Flytte

W is for WHISKY (NOT WHISKEY!)

Scotland's famous alcoholic spirit is always spelled without an "e" if it's distilled in Scotland. By the way, the word comes from the Gaelic *uisge beatha*, which means water of life.

X is for ST. ANDREW'S CROSS (X)

Scotland has two official flags:

- **The Saltire** - otherwise known as St. Andrew's cross, this flag has a white X on a blue background. (It makes up the blue background of the Union Jack*.)

- **The Royal Standard** - this is a yellow flag with a red lion rampant and red border. Everyone ignores the fact that it's only legally allowed to be used by royalty.

*The Union Jack might be the flag of the United Kingdom, but be wary of using it represent Scotland. This flag has complicated associations with sectarianism, and even racism. (You find the same attitude in England, where the St. George's Cross is often preferred.)

Y is for YANKS

All Americans are nicknamed Yanks in the UK, regardless of whether or not they think of themselves as Yankees. So, how do Scottish people *actually* feel about us Yanks? As individuals, we are generally well-received. Most Scots I've met, in fact, greet American visitors with open arms. They love our media and films, and a large segment of the population (particularly older) seems to have a real penchant for country music and dancing. Plus, the fact that so many of us just love Scotland and are extremely proud of our Scottish roots, if we have them, is kind of endearing to them.

Be forewarned however, that most Scots you meet really *don't* need to know that your great-great-great-great-great grandfather was a Campbell, or that you know your "family tartan". If you think that makes you a card-carrying Scot in their eyes, it really doesn't. Hate to break it to you, but unless you were actually born in Scotland, you will be seen as 100% American, always. Even if they're smiling and nodding as you're telling them about your "Scottish heritage", they're just being polite, because *all* Americans do this and they've heard it all before. Trust me on this!

Z is for (THE OTHER) Z

Once upon a time, there was an extra letter in the Scottish alphabet called yogh (ȝ). This obscure letter fizzled out when old printing presses substituted "ȝ" with a "z", which has a similar shape but sounds completely different. So, Mackenzie and Shetland are really supposed to be Mackenȝie and ȝetland.

2

the scottish character

*"Touch his head, and he will bargain and argue
with you to the last;
Touch his heart, and he falls upon your breast."*
- Andrew Carnegie on the Scottish character

Maybe I'm biased, but that saying is just so true.

Scots might have a gruff exterior, and maybe a fiery temper at times (think Groundskeeper Willie from *The Simpsons*.) You have to admit, there's something menacing about an angry Scottish accent. (Ever notice that they always make the bad guys Scottish?) After all, they are a nation of people descended from rugged, barefooted, freedom-loving Highland warriors who didn't have time for bullshit. But underneath it all, under all that stubbornness and grit... Scots are just big softies. They are friendly, loving, gregarious and heartwarming people.

Scots may be technically British. But the stiff upper lip? That must be an English thing. Unlike the English, Scots aren't afraid to strike up a friendly conversation with a stranger. At the same time, they are also a lot more likely to let you know exactly where you stand with them than their southern neighbors. This is a good thing, in my eyes. Nothing is worse than thinking someone is cool with you, until you find out later the opposite is true. Scots are expressive people who don't shy away from their emotions, and even veer toward sentimentality. The Scots I've known, especially the men, love to sing at any beer-fueled opportunity. They love their music passionately (and their sports teams too, of course.)

When you first meet one, they might come across as polite and reserved. But once they've warmed up to you, I'm pretty sure Scottish people love to talk more than anyone else on the planet — and I'm talking both men and women here. A get-together with pals can mean continuous back-and-forth *natter* or *blether* that extends into the wee hours of the morning — a lively hodgepodge of ranting, verbal jousting and lighthearted bickering. Scots are excellent storytellers too. When we speak to our Scottish family on Skype, we know we will require an uninterrupted block of three or four hours, or even more if allowed. That isn't because we haven't spoken in a while and we're catching up, that's just the normal length of a Scottish conversation amongst close friends and family.

One thing you learn early on about the Scots is that they are always up for a bit of banter. A major part of the Scottish sense of humor involves "taking the piss", or playfully poking fun at people. It's usually a sign of affection. Believe it or not, the more someone takes the piss out of you, the more they like you. (And of course they expect the same in return.) If someone is being overly polite and inoffensive, it's only because they don't yet feel comfortable enough around you.

The Scottish sense of humor in its purest form is offensive, twisted, self-deprecating, and dripping with sarcasm. (For a perfect example, watch clips of stand up comedian Kevin Bridges or Frankie Boyle.) It takes some getting used to, but the bottom line is, Scottish people don't like to take themselves too seriously, and don't like it when anyone else does either.

Are Scots a bit dour at times? Maybe. (Can you even say the word "dour" without thinking of a Scottish person?) The word, which means a sullen appearance or manner, even has Scottish origins — it comes from the Gaelic word *dúr*. It's true that you'll rarely see a Scot walking down the street with a grin on their face. Most of the time, they look pretty serious and frowny, at least in public. This lack of outward cheerfulness sure looks a lot like dourness, especially to us Americans. But it's not that the sour-faced Scots are necessarily dour, it's just that they're not hiding behind a mask of mandatory perkiness like we are. So, fellow Americans, enjoy giving your cheek muscles a rest in Scotland. People who are always smiling are regarded as kind of insane over there. That's not to say Scots don't smile (they smile quite a bit I might add), but you can rest assured it's sincere when they do.

As for the tightfisted stereotype, nothing could be further than the truth. Never have I met such generous people. Some Scots might be frugal, but that doesn't mean they're a nation of Scrooge McDucks. Scots aren't averse to a bit of materialism, and enjoy shopping, brand names and labels as much as we do. But they also have fewer things in general (there's nowhere to store it anyway, as you'll read about later). And they don't feel the push to constantly upgrade to the latest and greatest. Bigger is not necessarily better either, and if it ain't broke don't fix it. It's refreshing.

As an American, you'll also find it refreshing to be in a place where you aren't automatically asked, "So, what do you do?" within seconds of meeting someone. This is because what you do is not who you are in Scotland. Work is just a way to make money to do what you really want to do when you're not working. And, unlike here, Scots aren't always working. (They are required by law to have at least five weeks of vacation time and are generally allowed to take leave if needed, maternity or otherwise.) That's not to say Scottish people aren't hard workers. They work just as hard as Americans. They just have a better work-life balance to enjoy themselves, and to recover if they're not well — but most importantly, they don't feel guilty about it.

Scots are a deeply loyal lot. Beyond Scotland itself, they are loyal to their teams, their village, their pub, their family, and their friends. And with these deep loyalties come rivalries: Apart from the obvious one (England vs. Scotland), there's Teuchters vs. Sassenachs, Celtic vs. Rangers, Catholic vs. Protestant, Glasgow vs. Edinburgh, West End of Glasgow vs. East End of Glasgow, My Village vs. Your Village, My Pub vs. Your Pub, etc. But this loyalty also means you'll never have a more loyal friend than a Scot. If you have one, you're set for life. And if you move away and fall out of contact with a Scottish friend for years, or even decades, the moment you meet up again, you'll pick up right where you left off. There's a real deep devotion there that doesn't exist in the American culture of independence, where friends tend to come and go.

I'm not saying every Scot you meet is going to live up to all this. There are dicks everywhere — but thankfully, they're the exceptions to the rule.

3

things scottish people like

Before we begin, let me just state the obvious:
everyone is a unique individual, so not every Scottish person
is going to like *every single one* of these things — and some
may not like *any of them* at all. However, that doesn't mean
you can't get a pretty good idea of the social fabric of any
country based on shared culture and common experiences
— and the things that they tend to like.

SCOTTISH PEOPLE LIKE TEA.

The UK's obsession, and therefore Scotland's
obsession, with tea is no outdated stereotype. Nope. It might
not be drunk out of china cups with pinkies extended
anymore, but hot black tea (with milk and sugar, in varying
quantities) forms the very backbone of daily life in Scotland.

People drink mugs of it from the moment they wake
up, all the way until right before they go to bed at night.
Children are introduced to milked-down cups of it from a
very early age, so it is a comforting drink that most people
grow up with. The very first thing you'll be offered when
you arrive at someone's house is a "cuppa" (tea) because to
not offer it would actually be considered rude.

Tea serves any purpose someone might need it for at
any given moment. People use it to wake up, to calm down,

to celebrate, to commiserate, to cheer up, to warm up on a cold day, to rehydrate on a warm day, to fight boredom, or as a sleeping aid. It's both a social drink and a solitary drink. And everyone has their own established, very specific preference in terms of quantity of milk and sugar. Some take lots of milk and no sugar (like my husband), and some (like my mother-in-law) take lots of sugar and no milk. Some take neither milk nor sugar. But it's rare to find someone who take tea at all.

(Note: to add unnecessary confusion, in some households, the evening meal is also called tea. So in this case it would not be a hot drink, but dinner.)

SCOTTISH PEOPLE LIKE SAUSAGES.
Like, *really* like them. Sausages go above and beyond the breakfast table. They pop up everywhere, in all shapes and sizes.

There's **square sausage** (also called **lorne sausage** or **slice**) which is basically a rectangle of ground sausage meat. Then there's **black pudding** (a sausage not for the squeamish) made with actual pork blood mixed with oatmeal and other fillers. **White pudding** is like black pudding, but without the blood. Even **haggis** is a sausage in its own right. It's not unusual to find three or four of the sausages I just mentioned on a single breakfast plate.

A **sausage supper** is fried sausages served with chips (fries), one of the most popular fast food offerings (usually consumed late in an intoxicated state). A **roll and sausage** is what you call sausages between two rolls as a sandwich, and a *sausage roll* is a sausage baked in flaky pastry.

roll and sausage   **sausage roll**

In Scotland, *pigs in a blanket* are not hot dogs wrapped in pastry like they are here, but sausages wrapped in bacon. *Scotch eggs* are hard boiled eggs encased in sausage and breadcrumbs and deep fried.

Scottish sausages are a little thicker and have more filler than American sausages. (By filler, I mean things like rusk, crackers, crumbs, and onion). American sausages, in contrast, have less filler, but a much higher fat content. But the bottom line is, if you're in Scotland, expect sausages.

SCOTTISH PEOPLE LIKE TOAST.

People in Scotland have an obsession with putting things on slices of toasted bread and calling it a meal.

There is good reason for this: the average supermarket bread over there is simply amazing. We're not talking that sweetened, airy, sticks-to-the-roof-of-your-mouth mass produced stuff we get here in the States. The bread over there is hearty, dense and full of nutrition — and so big, it only fits halfway in the toaster!

Beans on toast is the cliche meal for broke 20-somethings, much like ramen is in the US. (By the way, baked beans are completely different over there. No brown sugar, no bacon-y or barbecue flavor. They are simply small white beans in a tomato sauce, similar to tomato soup.) There's also spaghetti on toast (from the tin), and egg on toast. Anything that would be good with toast is served not next to the toast, but right on top of the toast. Buttery toast with tea is even considered a complete meal on its own if someone is seriously stuck for meal ideas.

One of my favorite Scottish snacks is **cheese on toast**, also called **roasted cheese** or **toasted cheese** depending on who you ask. All you do is place thinly sliced cheddar cheese on slices of bread and put it under the grill (or broiler, as we would call it) until the cheese is bubbly and the bread is just slightly browned on the edges. It sounds so simple, but it's the perfect comfort food for a chilly climate. It's delicious on its own, but I highly recommend kicking it up a notch with Branston pickle (a pickled chutney). Leave it to the inventive Scots to get something so simple, so right.

A plate of roasted cheese with pickled chutney for dipping.

SCOTTISH PEOPLE LIKE IRN-BRU.

Pronounced *Iron Brew*, Irn-Bru is basically an orange-colored fizzy soft drink that tastes vaguely of bubblegum with a hint of iron shavings. Scottish people like this "brew" so much that it's officially known as "Scotland's other national drink". It's very important that you know of Irn-Bru's existence when you're in Scotland, if only for the fact it has a reputation for being the ultimate hangover cure.

SCOTTISH PEOPLE LIKE FITBA.

Fitba is Scots for football (what we call soccer). I can't stress enough how important football is to the majority of Scottish men. (I'm not being sexist here. Some women love it too, but it really is mostly men who take their obsession to the next level.) Nicknamed "the beautiful game", following your team is a lifelong passion for the "footie mad".

Scotland's national football team is nicknamed the Tartan Army. But within Scotland, there are many teams that compete against one another in the Scottish Premiership. There's Hearts of Midlothian (Edinburgh), Hibs (Edinburgh), Partick Thistle (Maryhill), and Ross County (Dingwall) — just to name a few.

But the biggest of these teams *by far* come out of Glasgow — Celtic and Rangers, collectively known as "The Old Firm", as I mentioned earlier. The rivalry between Celtic and Rangers is so fierce, that you'd be wise to avoid wearing anything associated with either of them, even as a tourist. (More on that later.)

SCOTTISH PEOPLE LIKE TO DRINK.

It might not be too much of a shock that Scots are fond of the *bevvy* (alcoholic beverages). That's just a fact. You could say that alcohol, and overindulging in said alcohol, is deeply in*grained* in Scottish culture, and has been for thousands of years.

Here are just a few ways to describe your state of inebriation in Scotland:

- *Aff yer tits*
- *Bevvied* (or *oan the bevvy*)
- *Blootered*
- *Guttered* (so drunk you could be lying in a gutter)
- *I'm oan it* ("I'm on my way to drunkenness")
- *Jaked* or *Jakied* (from "jakie", an insulting term for an alcoholic)
- *Mad wae it* (mad with it)
- *Minced*
- *Miraculous* (exceptionally drunk)
- *Oot yer dial*
- *Oot yer tree*
- *Paralytic*

- *Pished* (pissed in England)
- *Rat-arsed*
- *Rubbered*
- *Steamin'* (One of the most Glaswegian things you can say is *"Ah'm pure steamin'!"*)
- *Trollied*
- *Well on* (drunk and in the process of getting drunker)

While it *can* be said we Americans love to drink too, the level of excess usually peaks in college, after which we might be judged for having "a drinking problem". But once you step foot outside the US border, you discover it's all relative. In Scotland, what we would consider excessive drinking is much more acceptable for an entire lifetime.

You'll see 80 year old men knocking back pints at pubs on weekdays in broad daylight. It's acceptable to have few pints with coworkers at lunch every day. It's acceptable to polish off a bottle of wine every evening. It's even expected that fully grown adults will get falling-down drunk and "make an arse of themselves" on occasion, resting full blame on the booze afterwards. You can even get booze delivered to your door, like pizza, after the shops are shut. Apparently it's seen as that much of an "emergency" if you've run out that it needs to be available on speed dial.

Having said all this, there is one aspect of the Scottish drinking culture that puts us Americans to shame: driving under any influence at all, even one beer, is completely unacceptable, both legally and socially.

Not everyone in Scotland likes to drink, of course, but to say excessive drinking is not an enormous part of socializing in Scotland would be, well... a load of pish.

When it comes to participating in Scotland's drinking culture, there are a few subtleties to be aware of. When someone asks you to join them for a couple of pints, if you take them literally and leave after beer or two, they'll be left wondering what they said to offend you. A "pint or two", a "wee dram", a "wee hauf", a "wee swally" — all of these are invitations to get *pished* (inebriated). There's no better way to befriend a Scot than dropping your inhibitions a bit. This is when the bonds of true friendship are forged with them.

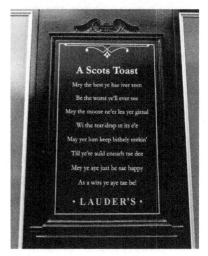

A night out with a group with the goal of drinking, unwinding and having a good time is called a *randan*. You can also say you're *on the sesh*. A *swally* is an alcoholic beverage. It's short for "a swallow of". If you want a drink (or ten) with someone, you could say, *"Fancy a wee swally?"* And the next day you might say, *"I cannae make it the day, mate. I overdid the swally last night.*

When Scots want a wee swally, they usually head to the *offie* (or the off-license, a shop licensed to sell alcohol "off" the premises of a licensed pub or bar) or the grocery store, and get a *carryout*.

Or, they can always just go to the pub.

SCOTTISH PEOPLE LIKE THEIR LOCAL PUB.

The local pub (often called just *the local*) is the traditional hub of Scottish socialization, so much so that you'll find one in almost every village or housing scheme, no matter how big or small.

Not to be confused with other types of pubs and bars, genuine locals are very clannish places where everyone knows everyone else and you wouldn't just walk into a random one without reason to be there.

A peek inside a local pub on the Isle of Arran.

Locals were once exclusively the domain of men, and even to this day, if you walk into one you'll find that women are still outnumbered. Instead of heading home after work every day, lots of men in generations past would head straight for the pub, their wives only ever seeing them in varying states of drunkenness afterwards. Pubs were literally a working man's second living room, a place to unwind from their grueling day jobs and socialize. Men's and women's lives in Scotland, particularly in industrial areas, were very separate up until fairly recently. (Women sadly had no equivalent, unless you count the *steamie*, which was the public washhouse. But that wasn't much of an escape.)

Thankfully, things have changed dramatically, which also means locals are falling out of favor as people prefer exploring the endless selection of trendy pubs, clubs and bars in "the toun" instead. Pub culture is still very much alive in that regard, it's just less restricted to any one place anymore (and therefore much less insular). But the stodgy old local remains as a lingering reminder of those old school days, even if the average age of the punters continues to rise. (If you want to take a closer look at what a pub in a housing scheme is like, the show *Still Game* has it covered in a hilarious way.)

SCOTTISH PEOPLE LIKE TO PARTY.
Coming from the land of bevvy and pubs, it's safe to say that Scottish people really know how to let their hair down. Any get-together can escalate into a full-blown celebration. Just watch. You'll see dancing, singing, cheering, embracing, etc.

Then there are the *ceilidhs*. Pronounced *kay-lee*, a ceilidh is basically a social gathering involving singing, dancing and Scottish folk music. In the more rural Highlands and Islands, ceilidhs are informal and usually held in someone's house. But in the rest of Scotland, they're organized affairs that take place in a hired venue, like a hotel or hall.

But for the ultimate demonstration of Scotland's love of partying, look no further than Hogmanay (New Year's Eve). Nobody celebrates that holiday harder or better than the Scots. Let's also not forget to mention the many music festivals. Or the vibrant nightlife in cities. There are Engagement Parties, followed by Stag Do's and Hen Do's (bachelor and bachelorette parties). Then there are the weddings. Weddings are huge. Anniversary parties, 21st birthday parties, 40th birthday parties, 80th birthday parties. Even funerals are great big parties. Bottom line is, Scots just *love* to celebrate, and just about any excuse will do.

SCOTTISH PEOPLE LIKE SNOOKER.

Snooker looks a lot like the game of pool, but it isn't. It's played on a much bigger table with smaller pockets and different rules altogether. It's a game traditionally associated with slobbish, beer-gutted pubgoers. I've been told that in the 1980s, it was normal for all professional snooker players to chain-smoke and get trashed on pints of beer as they played on live TV, which was half the fun of watching it. (Just look up Bill Werbeniuk.)

SCOTTISH PEOPLE LIKE THE BOOKIES.

Betting is a popular pastime in Scotland. Many villages have a bookies, often cleverly located near the pub. You can bet on many things, like football results, but among the most popular is horse racing. When you *put a line on*, that means you're placing a bet.

SCOTTISH PEOPLE LIKE HILL CLIMBING (MUNRO BAGGING).

Scotland is a very hilly country, especially the further north you go (they're called the Highlands for a reason). Munros are mountains that are over 3,000 feet high, and for more athletically-inclined Scots, climbing as many of these natural features as possible (*munro bagging*) is a popular hobby.

SCOTTISH PEOPLE LIKE THEIR TV.

It's my guess that Scottish people like to watch TV *a lot* more than most Americans these days, and for good reason. First of all, the television set was invented in Scotland, so why not? Second, the constant miserable weather makes it all too easy to stay indoors. And third, Scottish TV is actually somewhat watchable. For one, there are far fewer adverts (commercials). I've watched episodes of my favorite American shows in Scotland and been surprised by extra scenes that I never knew existed because they were always cut to air more commercials. And cringey ads for prescription drugs and ambulance-chasing lawyers are illegal, thankfully. A few channels, like BBC Scotland, don't have any ads at all.

Scottish people love their quiz shows, talent competitions, reality shows, sports, and fly-on-the-wall documentaries. They have some top notch comedies too.

But they especially need their TV if they follow the soaps. In case you didn't already know, soaps are *huge* in the UK, almost as essential to life as tea for some folks, and I'm talking both men and women of all ages.

People who watch soaps invest years in keeping up with the fast-paced storylines, so for that reason it's almost impossible to catch up if you want to start watching one. Part of the appeal is that the characters in these shows all look "real" and they have "real" problems that make the average viewer feel better about their own life. To sum it up: American soaps are glossy and cheesy; British soaps are gritty and sleazy. *River City* is Scotland's answer to England's *Coronation Street ("Corrie"), Eastenders, Emmerdale,* and *Hollyoaks.*

SCOTTISH PEOPLE LIKE GOLF.

You can't write a book about the birthplace of golf and not mention golf. (The sport was invented in the seaside town of St. Andrews on the northeast coast.)

And yes, Scottish people (particularly men) of all ages play it, often regularly. They also will play it regardless of weather — otherwise they'd never play at all. If the golf course is covered in snow, they just use a bright orange ball instead of the usual white one.

SCOTTISH PEOPLE LIKE (A DIFFERENT KIND OF) BOWLING

Scots love their ten-pin bowling alleys too. But there's another completely different kind of bowling in Scotland called lawn bowls (outside) or carpet bowls (inside). Like ten-pin bowling, it's played by rolling balls along the floor or ground, but that's pretty much where the similarities end.

SCOTTISH PEOPLE LIKE BEING SCOTTISH.

Scots have a complicated relationship with their homeland. They may be quick to criticize it, but they'll be even quicker to take offense if an outsider does the same. Scottish people can be a sentimental bunch (especially after a few drinks), but nobody makes fun of themselves more than they do. Not even the English.

4

how to speak scottish

THAT ACCENT

We Americans love a good Scottish accent. But Scotland, for being a tiny country, is actually a land of *many* accents. There is no such thing as *the* Scottish accent because there are hundreds of Scottish accents, and they vary from region to region even by a number of miles. Part of my husband's family lives in Stirling, and it's amazing how differently they speak, even though they live a couple dozen miles away from his family in Glasgow.

One thing all Scottish accents share, however, is rhotacism, which means they always pronounce their "R's". (You've probably noticed the English do not.) For those of us who go a bit weak in the knees hearing those rolled Scottish Rs, this is a very nice thing indeed.

THE PATTER

If you're visiting Scotland for the first time, you might have a *wee* bit of trouble understanding those around you at first. But set foot anywhere near the city of Glasgow, and that's when the shit hits the fan. You'll probably find yourself saying "What???!" more times in one day than you have in your entire lifetime, at least in the very beginning. It might give you a **beamer** (red face), but Glaswegians expect this. They see it as part of the running joke that nobody outside of Scotland can understand them.

Don't feel too bad though, because the working class Glasgow dialect (known as the *patter*) is so unintelligible that Glaswegian shows are subtitled for audiences in the rest of the UK. When you reach the point where you're finally fluent in the patter, it's as good as mastering a foreign language. (Because, let's face it, it really doesn't sound much like English at all.)

Here are a few reasons why, if you're in Glasgow, you're having a hard time understanding people:

- The short "i" sounds like a short "e" sound. So, "six" becomes "sex", which can lead to some confusion.
- The letter "J" is pronounced "jie" (rhymes with tie)
- The number "one" is pronounced "wan" (or sometimes "yin")
- I - *Ah*
- I am - *Am are*
- My - *ma*
- All - *Aw*
- On - *oan*
- Cold and hold become *caud* and *haud*. *"Haud oan, I've got a caud."*
- Do - *dae*
- To - *tae*
- From - *fae*
- Those - *thae*
- Stand - *staun*
- Understand - *unnerstaun*
- Most - *maist*
- Head and bread become *heid* and *breid*
- More - *mair*
- Give me - *gies* (pronounced like geeze with a hard g)

- Clothes - *claes* (sounds exactly like clays. This one really got me in the beginning.)
- Will not, is not, didn't, wouldn't, shouldn't become *willnae, isnae, didnae, wouldnae, shouldnae,* and so forth.
- You, plural - *yous*
- Why - *how* ("Why not?" - *"How no?"*)
- What???! - *whit???!* (Exactly.)

Other unique features of the Glasgow dialect include starting sentences with the word "see" to introduce a subject of conversation. *"See ma sister? She disnae like him."* And, at the end of sentences, adding "but", which is similar to "though". *"I like him. I'd never trust him but."*

If all this doesn't make your head spin, imagine it all coming at you at warp speed, mixed with generous helpings of in-jokes and slang. As you can see, it is almost designed to trip you up. Seriously.

So what hope does an American have of ever understanding the patter if it's so... not understandable? I found the best and fastest way to become fluent (other than having a Scottish family) is to watch Scottish TV shows *with the subtitles on.* I honestly think that's how I finally became "bilingual". *Still Game, Chewin' the Fat,* and *Burnistoun* are good places to start (they all happen to be on Netflix right now). Not only do you pick up on the language, but you get a peek at real, unsanitized Scottish culture too, in a very entertaining way.

JUST FOR FUN...
Say "Space Ghetto" in your normal American accent. You've just said "Spice Girl" in a perfect Glasgow accent, with no effort at all on your part!

PROFANITY, EXPLETIVES AND FOUR LETTER WORDS

One thing you'll come to realize is that Scots really fucking love swearing. Swear words are like commas to the Scots. In casual conversation, "fuckin'" might punctuate every sentence, multiple times. Even though it makes Scottish people sound like they're always angry about something, it's actually harmless and meaningless — and so reflexive on their part, that you'll soon not notice it anymore either.

A word of warning, though: the "c-word" basically translates to "guy", which *does* takes some getting used to. It's a schizophrenic word that can either be used neutrally, affectionately or insultingly depending on the context. While "cunt" is not exactly used in polite company, it just doesn't carry the same level of extreme offense that it does in the States. (Kind of like how "bastard" is about as offensive as the word jerk to us, but in the UK it's a *huge* insult.)

GREETINGS & PLEASANTRIES

So now that we've gotten swearing out of the way, let's move on to the basics of everyday polite conversation in Scotland.

- *Hiya!* - A cheerful greeting, usually said in a sing-songy voice.
- *Awrite?* - The more Glaswegian way of saying hi is the shortened version of "Are you alright?" It's confusing, but you're not actually being asked if you're alright, so the correct response isn't yes or no — just greet them right back with a hi or whatever. I know it defies all logic, but trust me on this.
- *Cheerio!* - A cheerful way of saying "goodbye". If you want to kick the cheerfulness up a notch, you say *Cheery-bye!*
- *Cheers* (or *Ta*) - A quick thanks you'd give, for example, when someone holds the door open for you or hands you a cup of tea.

- *Aye* - The preferred method of saying "yes".
- *Naw* - An alternative to "no".

TERMS OF ENDEARMENT

Your friends are your *mates* or *pals*. (But anyone can be called pal, really. It's often used to address strangers of either gender.) A guy's pals will usually have affectionately descriptive nicknames, like "Big Lee" or "Fat Boab" or "Wee Rab". Nicknames are a really big thing in Scotland and they stick with you for a lifetime.

If you're a woman, get used to being called *doll, hen* or *pet*, especially by women older than you are. It's the equivalent of sweetheart or honey. An older woman might be called an *old dear*, or if you want to go old school, *wifie*. For the most part, girls (and young women) are still called *lassies*, and boys are *laddies*.

Young men are called *son*, even if they are in no way related to the speaker. A big guy might be called *Big Yin* (big one). Likewise, an older guy might be called *Auldjin* (old one).

If you're in a relationship, your girlfriend is your *burd*, and your boyfriend is your *man*.

INSULTS

Insulting terms vastly outnumber nice ones in the Scottish vocabulary. Usually when a Scot hurls an insult at you they'll stick the word "ya" in front of it for that personal touch. Example: *"Ya bastard!"*

Insults can be deceiving though. As mentioned earlier, the more someone takes the piss out of you, *the more they like you*. Therefore, what sounds like nasty stream of unpleasantries might very well just be friends exchanging greetings. Example: *"Awright ya wee bawbag?"* translates to "how are you doing, my friend?" But drop the "awright", and *"Haw you, ya bawbag"* means someone is about to get it. It's all about the tone.

A word of warning: if your name is Fanny and you're going anywhere *near* Scotland, consider a legal name change. Seriously. Fanny is not and never has been a grandmotherly word for bottom in the UK. It's slang for female genitalia. Scotland takes this a step further than England and uses fanny as pretty much their stock insult for anyone at any time. *"Ya fanny."* *"Fanny baws."* So yeah, look into that name change.

Here are a few more stock Scottish insults:

- **Biddy** or **old boot** - Insulting terms for an unpleasant old woman.
- **Nippy sweetie** - Woman with a sharp tongue and attitude to match.
- **Wrang yin** - Someone who is "wrong in the head", capable of cruel and reprehensible behavior
- **Wido** - Someone who has done something **wide** (shocking and inappropriate).
- **Hairy** - A haggard, promiscuous young woman who is rough around the edges.
- **Hackit** - Just plain ugly.
- **Bauldie** - A bald man. (Usually followed by "bastard".)
- **Speccy** - Someone who wears specs (glasses).
- **Glaikit** - Spaced out, with a vacant look on your face
- **Sweetiewife** - A man who likes to gossip.

- **Radge** - Someone who is mentally unstable (used in the Edinburgh area).
- **Roaster** - Someone who is making a complete jackass of themselves and getting on your nerves. *"Aye he's a roaster, right enough."* Along these lines, another word for a roaster is a *warmer*.
- **Nae-use-r** - Someone who is "no use" to anyone, with nothing to offer society
- **Nyaff** - A small, worthless person.

Other choice insults selected for your perusal include **Bawbag** (scrotum), **Bawheid** (ballhead), **Balloon** (someone full of hot air), **Dafty, Doughball, Eejit, Fud, Numpty, Rocket**, and **Wallaper.**

Please note: Scots are *very* creative when it comes to insults, and for that reason you're not limited to any of these. *Any* word you can think of is fair game, and the more random the better. A few years ago, a man at my father-in-law's pub called his pal a "Bovril" (Bovril being a brand of salty meat paste.) This was taken as such an insult that it almost started a brawl. I can guarantee that was the first and possibly last time Bovril has ever been used as an insult in the history of Scotland, but the point is, the more unexpected the word is to the recipient, the more insulting it is.

EXPRESSIONS OF JOY
Scots are a spirited bunch, so when they're actually happy about something they'll let you know about it.
- **Ya dancer!** - A phrase used when experiencing luck or good fortune.
- **Belter!** - A multipurpose word that can mean "wow", "awesome!", or "I agree emphatically!" Something can even *be* a belter if it's really great. *"It was a belter!"*

- *Ya beauty!* - Fantastic!
- *Yaldi!* - Awesome!
- *Here we, here we, here we fuckin' go!* - Usually chanted by groups of people in varying states of inebriation.
- *That's smashin'!*

EXPRESSIONS OF ANGER

And then, when the "Angry Scotsman" makes an appearance, you'll likely hear any one of the following phrases.

- *Git it up ye!* - an insult used to rub in a victory you've had over someone
- *Git it right roond ye!* - used when you have beaten someone or conquered something
- *Git tae fuck!* - Get out of my sight!
- *Ah ya bastard!* - Ouch! or Dammit!
- *Aye, right!* - Yeah, sure! (sarcastic response to a question or to challenge a presumption)
- *Away and bile yer heid!* - "Go away and boil your head!"
- *Moan'en!* - C'mon then! (an invitation to battle)

A *square go* is a one-on-one fight, with no weapons. And, in the Glasgow area, when someone looks angry, you might say they have a *face like fizz*.

EXPRESSIONS OF DISGUST

The Scots have quite a few words to describe things that disgust them. If you're disgusted by someone or something, you can say it *"Gives me the boak"*, which means it makes you want to vomit. If something gives you the *dry boak* (dry heaves), that's even worse. Something that smells really bad is *honkin'*. And *midden*, an old word for the communal garbage dump, is used to describe anything that's equally disgusting.

A few more words to describe your disgust include *Boggin', Bowffin', Clatty, Manky, Mingin',* and *Mawkit.*

...AND FINALLY, SOME BRILLIANT SCOTTISH SAYINGS.

Scots are quite the chatty bunch, and as a result, they've accumulated several centuries' worth of quips and quotations. I could literally fill a whole new book with nothing *but* Scottish sayings, so I've selected a few favorites.

Scottish Saying	*Translation*
"Dinna fash yersel."	Don't worry about it.
"You must think I button up the back."	You must think you can get one past me; that I'm gullible.
"What's for ye won't pass ye by."	Que sera sera. Whatever will be will be.
"We're all Jock Tamson's bairns."	We're all from the same stock; in the end nobody is better than anyone else.
"If he fell into the Clyde, he'd come out with a salmon in his mouth."	He always falls ass-backward into enviable situations. (Refers to the River Clyde in Glasgow.)
"It's a braw bricht moonlicht nicht th' nicht."	It's a nice bright moonlit night tonight.
"If he was chocolate, he'd eat himself."	He's really full of himself.
"Back to auld claes and porridge."	Party's over. Back to reality. (Usually said after holidays.)

"Lang may yer lum reek."

Long may your chimney smoke.
Here's hoping you have a long life.

"Here's tae us! Wha's like us?
...Damn few, and they're a' deid!"

"Here's to us; who's as good as us?
Damn few, and they're all dead!" –
a classic, traditional Scottish toast.
(Drunken sentimentality at its
finest.)

5

the scourges of scotland: things you might not like so much

"It's SHITE being Scottish! We're the lowest of the low. The scum of the fucking Earth! The most wretched, miserable, servile, pathetic trash that was ever shat into civilization. Some hate the English. I don't. They're just wankers. We, on the other hand, are COLONIZED by wankers. Can't even find a decent culture to be colonized BY. We're ruled by effete assholes. It's a SHITE state of affairs to be in, Tommy, and ALL the fresh air in the world won't make any fucking difference!"

- Renton in "Trainspotting"

I've lived in many places, and *nowhere* is perfect by a long shot... but Scotland does come pretty close. However, to keep this book as authentic to real-life experience as possible, I felt it was important to compile a list of some of the most common gripes people have about day-to-day life in Scotland.

THE CLIMATE.

Dreich is the Scots word used to describe their infamous dreary, cold, all-around miserable weather.

You've probably also heard that it rains a lot in Scotland. Newsflash: that's true. In Glasgow, you'll often hear people say *"it's pishin doon"* ("it's raining"), because... well, it usually is. But guess what else? I have never ruined more umbrellas that I did when I lived in Glasgow. Scotland is also a very windy place — it's actually the windiest country in Europe. It's a very common sight to see inverted umbrellas littering the streets. For that reason, you often have no other choice than to get simultaneously soaked and windblasted the moment you step outside. (I  honestly don't know how Scottish women look so put together most of the time.)

You might read this and think, "Suits me! I love rain and will feel right at home in a drizzly climate." But it's not just the overabundance of rain, but the astounding lack of sunshine that torments even those who have lived in Scotland their entire lives. (And the reason why everyone goes for cheap weekend breaks to sunny Spain.) Because the sun is so rarely seen, Scottish people joke that they're so pale they're almost a shade of blue. For this reason, you'll notice there's a pandemic of tanning salons in towns and cities, which are hugely popular with both men and women alike.

When it's not rainy, it's probably overcast. Just look at the five day forecast for locations in Scotland to see what I mean, especially in the colder months. Nowhere in America has fewer hours of sunlight in a year, by a long shot.

And if the climate isn't maddening enough...

NEDS.

Ask any Scot one thing they hate about their country, and they'll usually say *neds*. Neds are pretty much young hooligans or petty criminals with a profound lack of respect for anyone or anything. ("Ned" is short for either "ne'r-do-well" or "non-educated delinquent", depending on who you ask.) A female ned is sometimes called a **senga**. (Senga is an old-fashioned Scottish name; Agnes spelled backwards. Why it now means female ned, I'm not sure.) The rough equivalent in England is the "chav". In Ireland it's the "knacker".

A "squad" of potential young neds (sometimes called neds-in-training) in Glasgow.

Unfortunately, neds are a huge social problem in urban areas and beyond that for some reason the **polis** (police) don't have much of a handle on, even though we're talking about teenagers here. They are responsible for widespread property damage, like setting things on fire and smashing windows, and random physical violence, stemming from a toxic combination of boredom and inebriation, usually having something to do with Buckfast tonic wine (Don't worry, I'll get into that next.)

Because neds are usually nothing more than scrawny kids below legal drinking age, they use strength in numbers, so they travel in groups. These groups even appoint themselves with team names and logos, usually the name of their village ending with the word "Fleeto", "Squad" or "Young Team". You can find their poorly executed *menchies* (graffiti) scrawled in permanent marker or scratched on bus shelters and the like, further degenerating any environment they inhabit.

(In David Attenborough voice): Neds have left their primitive markings on this bus shelter.

If you come across a group of neds, it's best to just ignore them and don't interact. It's just not worth it.

BUCKFAST.

Buckfast, nicknamed "Buckie", is a fortified wine created by monks at Buckfast Abbey in Devon, England a century ago for medicinal purposes, supposedly to cure malaise. It all sounds so wholesome, doesn't it? But its other nickname, "wreck the hoose juice" gives you the first clue that it's anything but. As the saying goes, *"Buckfast: the drink that gets you fucked fast."* It's cheap, has a 15% alcohol content, and the caffeine of about six cups of coffee. Drinking Buckie is a sort of antisocial badge of honor for neds, and it's become almost the symbol of neddy culture. The one time I tried it, my palate detected the delicate flavor and consistency of over-the-counter cough syrup.

There's an area called the "Buckfast Triangle" in the East End (the rougher part) of greater Glasgow, between Airdrie, Coatbridge and Bellshill, where Buckie sales (and the high crime rates and antisocial behavior that go along with them) are highest. You'd probably be advised to avoid setting foot in this triangle unless you have a pretty compelling reason to be there.

BEASTIES.

"Wee sleekit, cow'rin, tim'rous beastie" is a famous line in a Robert Burns poem about a mouse. Beasties are bugs or other small creatures. For this section, we're going to focus on insects.

And when you think of Scottish insects, the first one that should probably come to mind is the midge, a teeny tiny bloodthirsty gnat that thrives in the damp Scottish countryside. It's almost as if Scotland had too much natural beauty, so something had to come and level the playing field a bit. Midges have the uncanny ability to ruin any attempt at enjoying the countryside for any length of time, like camping for example. They swarm in clouds and their bites leave small, irritating red bumps.

And, if you're an arachnophobe, you might not be too pleased to hear that Scottish house spiders are frickin' huge. My husband refers to them as hairy hands. They are the kind of spider that make you jump out of your skin when you come across one: hideous, hairy things with long, thick legs that look like they belong in the Amazon, not in a Scottish house. There's a legend that these hairy-legged horrors were imported via a shipment of bananas, but who knows if that's true.

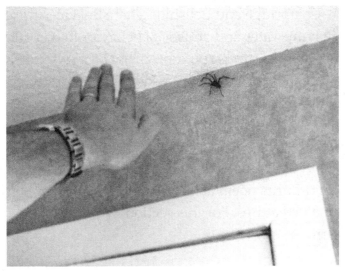

A moderately sized Scottish "house spider". (Oh yes, they get bigger than this.)

If that's not enough, in September, you might want to be on your guard for wasps. It's true that wasps all over the world go a little stinger-happy in early autumn when they know their days are numbered. But in Scotland, they are a new level of crazy. And they are aggressive little bastards. They seem to actively make a point of going for you, even if you're nowhere near them. For someone who has a wasp phobia like myself, this is a living nightmare. Give me a hairy hand any day.

RUBBISH, RUBBISH EVERYWHERE.

I'm always surprised how much litter there is on the ground in populated areas. That, and people for the most part seem a lot less willing or likely to pick up after their dogs. You always have to watch your feet as you're walking, or you'll end up with a smelly surprise on your shoe. And let's just say it's not unusual to see puddles of vomit on city streets, especially after a Friday or Saturday night. (There's a reason nobody wears open-toed shoes, even when it's *not* raining.)

URBAN POVERTY.

"The Ugly Truth" is that not all of Scotland is scenic.

Scotland was recently named the most beautiful country in the world, and I can't argue with that... as long as you're talking about the parts of the country that are far away from certain urban areas. Unfortunately, there are pockets of poverty in Scotland's cities that you're definitely better off avoiding. Not only are they the opposite of beautiful (and that's an understatement), but they're not exactly safe either. That's not to say you should avoid Scotland's cities, because they're fantastic — just stick to the city centre and touristy areas. You're not missing out in life, for example, if you never see Easterhouse, Cumbernauld (a.k.a. Scumbernauld), or Drumchapel (a.k.a. Little Beirut). Believe me.

CASUAL RACISM.

Scotland prides itself on being a tolerant, welcoming and forward-thinking country, and it genuinely is. However, the general population (and even the media) might be a bit less PC than we are are used to. Because of our loaded racial history in America, anything that even hints at racism is completely off-limits, unless you want to be tarred and feathered by society.

But in Scotland, you might be caught off guard the first time you overhear someone calling a Chinese restaurant "the Chinky's". Or when you hear the corner shop being referred to as the "Paki shop" (Paki is a slur for Pakistani, and most convenience store owners are in fact West Asian.) But as shocking as this sounds to the average American, most casual racism is not intended to be mean-spirited, as it might be Stateside. You can blame it on how people were brought up, especially if they grew up back in the days when it was rare to see anyone in Scotland who wasn't Scottish. Thankfully, the vast majority of people know better nowadays and it's becoming increasingly uncommon.

SECTARIANISM, VIOLENCE & FOOTBALL.

The Red Sox vs Yankees rivalry? Cute. The Celtic vs Rangers rivalry? Not cute. People literally *die*. A lot of pubs in rougher parts of Glasgow have a sign on the door saying "No football colours allowed". This is because Glasgow is a city where walking into the wrong pub wearing the wrong football jersey can actually trigger a brawl, or at the very least, a "Glasgow Kiss" (headbutt). Or worse. Glasgow has long been known as a murder capital of Europe, and incidents of violence and domestic abuse escalate on days when an Old Firm game takes place. Why does this happen? Sectarianism.

Seriously, for such a modern country, you'd be surprised that Scotland still has Catholic vs. Protestant issues lurking in its underbelly, bizarrely reinforced through football: Celtic is for Catholics and Rangers is for Protestants. So, not only are the two main rival sports fans divided by team, but they are divided by their presumed religion too.

And you might be surprised to find out that students in *public* school are still segregated by religion. There are Catholic Schools and Protestant Schools. Sometimes the schools share the same building, but the students are still kept separate with different entrances and exits. Catholic school children might disparagingly call Protestant school children "Proddies", and are called "Fenian bastards" in return. This artificial divide in schooling makes them see one another as different from a very young age.

Weird reminders of Catholicism vs. Protestantism exist in unexpected ways. You could be sitting in your house on any given day and hear a drumbeat approaching, and when you look out the window, you'll see a parade of people holding banners saying "Orange Pride". This is the Orange Walk, march held by the Orangemen, a Protestant pride group.

The good thing is, while all this obsession with religion is off putting, it actually doesn't reflect on the country as a whole. Scotland is a very secular country, much more so than the US. Your religion doesn't matter in day-to-day life or interactions, and most people don't bother going to church or chapel at all. But the dark cloud of sectarianism does cast a shadow, and creates divides where there really shouldn't be anymore.

6

101 things i love about scotland: my personal list

"If it's not Scottish, it's crap!"
- Stuart Rankin, Saturday Night Live

One of the great things about Scotland is that for every complaint you could possibly have about it, you can always find something else that will more than make up for it. Here is my own personal list of "loves", from what I've seen and experienced so far. I hope they inspire you, too!

1. First of all, *this* is typical **Scottish scenery** (complete with castle ruins).

2. Speaking of **castles**, there are over 3,000 in Scotland.
3. You'll often see *"Céad míle fáilte"* (pronounced *kee-ut mee-luh fah-ill-tya*) on place name signs for towns and cities. It's Gaelic for *a hundred thousand welcomes*. It's true, you really do feel welcome in Scotland, because the people are simply the best.

4. *Gaelic signage*, especially the further north you go.
5. All lakes in Scotland are called *lochs*, and there are over 30,000 to choose from.
6. There are *only 5 million people*, just 8.5% of the UK's population.
7. Out of over 790 islands, only around 100 are inhabited. (A tiny rock island unfit for habitation is called a *skerry*.)
8. The *Caledonian MacBrayne* (nicknamed CalMac) ferry is always ready to transport you to whichever habited island you choose.

9. Scotland is only the size of Maine, so *everything is relatively close by.* (You can drive forever and ever in the US and only get through a few states.)
10. This is what it looks like out your window when you go on *road trips* in Scotland:

11. Scotland has the *highest mountain* in the British Isles, Ben Nevis.
12. In the Highlands there's a *waterfall three times higher than Niagara Falls*, called Eas a' Chual Aluinn which means "waterfall of the beautiful tresses".

13. **Standing stones**, just standing there in the middle of fields. You can literally walk out to them and touch ancient history. No need to go to Stonehenge.

14. Scotland's **"right to roam"** means you can walk anywhere.
15. The place is **green**, year round.
16. More rain means many more **rainbows**.
17. **Stone fences.**
18. **Stags.**
19. In the Highlands, the only traffic jams are **sheep in the road**.
20. **Highland cows** (or coos, as they say) with shaggy orange hair over their eyes. Need I say more?

21. **Tiny daisies** growing wild in the grass.
22. **Hedgehogs.**
23. **Foxes.**
24. **Scottish salmon.** (And smoked salmon sandwiches.)
25. **Merry Dancers**, a.k.a. the Northern Lights (aurora borealis).
26. **Dramatic clouds.**
27. **Shetland ponies.**

28. *Sheep.* Fluffy sheep in every field
29. *Puffins* on rocky shores
30. Forest floors are carpeted in **green moss.**
31. Sometimes they're carpeted in **bluebell flowers** too, and it doesn't get more beautiful than that.
32. *Smirr* is a soft, mist-like rain — a lot more common in Scotland than the drenching downpours we get.
33. Speaking of *mist*, there's no shortage of that, and it's hauntingly beautiful.
34. The *Electric Brae*, a stretch of road where your car appears to be rolling uphill.
35. The *architecture* in cities is amazing, even if you're not someone who normally appreciates it. Look up anywhere in Glasgow, and you'll see grimacing gargoyles and human statues "propping up" buildings.
36. The *sense of history* everywhere. (Yes, it's cliche, but you can really feel it.)
37. Scotland's motto is *"no one provokes me with impunity"* (in Latin). That says a lot right there.
38. *The haar* is a chilly sea fog that blows in from the North Sea on pleasant days between the months of April and September, causing temperatures to drop suddenly. It might not be very lovable, but it's a great word nonetheless.
39. The chilly wet weather might be a downer, but it gives you plenty of opportunities to *coorie in* by the fire.
40. Black coal soot still on buildings in cities, a gritty reminder of their industrial past.

41. **Magpies,** which are like scarily intelligent black and white crows. As the nursery rhyme goes, *"One for sorrow, Two for joy. Three for a girl, Four for a boy. Five for silver, six for gold. Seven for a secret never to be told."*

42. **Seagulls** are a major fixture in landlocked Scottish cities alongside pigeons. Most people would say they're an annoyance, but I think it's a unique problem. Supposedly they're attracted to the endless supply of half-eaten fish suppers dropped by seas of bevvied revelers, coming in and going out like the tide.

43. A *paddock* is an old Scottish word for a frog. For some reason, I love this.

44. **Blue tits.** (I know, I know, the name, right? Haha.) But they are adorable blue and yellow songbirds.

45. **Heather.** Like thistle, it's another rugged purple flower symbolic of Scotland, carpeting the country's sprawling landscapes. And white heather is considered lucky.

46. **Windy streets** in cities. (In both senses of the word!)

47. City centers with **wide, walkable streets** where no cars are allowed.

48. Real *fish and chips* right by the seaside.

49. High quality **TV** with far fewer commercials.

50. **People on TV** don't look perfect.

51. There are some great **Scottish place names**. Dull, Eigg, Yell, Dufftown, Muck, Dingwall, Troon, Insch, Wigtown, Uig. And that's only a few.

52. Every so often, the Duke of Wellington statue outside the Glasgow Museum of Modern Art has a **traffic cone "hat"**. Nobody knows exactly who does it, but it's been happening since the 1980s.

53. **Winching**, a great word for a French kiss or full-on makeout session. If you ever pass through Buchanan Bus Station in Glasgow, you'll see a bronze sculpture of a couple kissing that has the name "Winchers' Stance". Fun fact: winch comes from wench (as in woman), so if you were seeing a woman, you were wenchin'. (Nice, huh?)

54. **Chicken tikka masala.** Scotland is the birthplace of this Indian food classic.

55. You can usually find a **tea room** somewhere, whether you're in the city or way out in a remote village.

56. **White cottages** on hillsides.

57. Abundance of reasonable lodging, like **bed & breakfasts (or B&Bs)** — which range from a spare room in somebody's house to a spacious, modern guesthouse.

58. **The shopping.** Glasgow has more shops than anywhere in the UK, besides London.

59. **Nightlife.** The choices for how to spend your Friday and Saturday night in Edinburgh or Glasgow are endless.

60. Speaking of nightlife, **"goin' to the dancin'"** means going to a nightclub, and I love that.

61. **Bike rides** through the countryside.

62. The **Corryvreckan Whirlpool,** the third largest whirlpool in the world.

63. **Skara Brae** village in Orkney, dating back to 3,180 BC, is older than the Pyramids.

64. Britain's **oldest tree**, the Fortingall Yew, which is thousands of years old.

65. *Isle of Arran* is Scotland in miniature. It has a castle, standing stones, Highland cows, waterfalls, forests, and a mountain all in one place. (If you're short on time, just go there.)

66. Plenty of mythological creatures to tap into your imagination, like the *Selkie*, the *Brownie*, the *Kelpie*, and of course *Nessie* (the famous Loch Ness Monster).

67. Legends like that of *Sawney Bean*, a cannibal who lived in a sea cave with his large human-flesh-eating family hundreds of years ago, to give you the creeps whenever you visit a remote beach in Scotland. (It was the inspiration for the Wes Craven film "The Hills Have Eyes".)

68. Speaking of *beaches*, they're magical in Scotland.

69. *The Broons* and *Oor Wullie*, beloved comic strips posted in the Sunday Post continuously since 1936.

70. The *ghost stories*. There's a supernatural element to Scotland that I just love.

71. The *cemeteries*.

72. *Pub culture*.

73. The *tap water* is soft in most places, meaning your hair (and everything else) washes cleaner. It tastes great too.

74. *Distilleries* (even if you're not a fan of whisky, they're fun to visit).

75. *The food* is cheaper. And it's high quality, less processed (there are stricter guidelines about what's allowed in food) and usually local.

76. For some reason, some Scottish *candy names are hilarious* — strippit baws, granny sookers, lucky tatties, soor plooms.

77. *Oban*, a small but charming seaside town.

78. Scotland produces some serious *musical talent* for a tiny country — Hue & Cry, The Proclaimers, Franz Ferdinand, Garbage, Simple Minds, Deacon Blue, Bay City Rollers, Biffy Clyro, Snow Patrol — just to name a few.

79. *Music festivals*, the weekend kind where you camp out in tents in farmers' fields. I went to the Wickerman Festival (RIP) and T in the Park two years in a row.

80. The sound of *bagpipes*.

81. Whether you call it a brogue or a burr, any *Scottish accent* is gorgeous all the same. Yes, I even include Glasgow in that. (So many Americans have said to my husband, "I could listen to you all day.")

82. *Men in kilts.* Yes.

83. *Words in everyday speech*, like "aye" and "wee", "laddie" and "lassie".

84. The romance of **Loch Lomond** and the associated song.
85. **Robert Burns** and how much a poet is revered.
86. Thanks to the Gulf Stream, it's mild enough that **palm trees** grow, especially along the west coast.

87. Edinburgh's annual **Fringe Festival** features famous celebrities, artists, musicians, and stand-up comedians. People from all over the UK (and worldwide) flock to it every August, meaning it gets very crowded. (I guess you could say it's "hoachin'".)
88. **Isle of Skye.** One of the most beautiful places in all the world.
89. **Glencoe.** Another one of the most beautiful places in all the world.
90. The rapid-fire, droll **sense of humor** and the fact nobody takes themselves too seriously.
91. The slower **pace of life**.
92. The utmost importance of **family**.
93. Paying for **healthcare** is not a concern.
94. The people are humorously **self-deprecating** and don't brag.
95. **Public transportation.** You can get away with not having a car.
96. **Travel.** The rest of Europe is just a quick, cheap flight away.
97. People are **less materialistic** in general. They are happy with fewer things.
98. How such a tiny country with a low population has had such an **outsized influence on the modern world.**
99. The city of **Glasgow**. Edinburgh may be considered Glasgow's pretty sister, but it IS very touristy. Glasgow is a bit more rough around the edges and definitely has a more authentic character. (Of course, I'm totally biased.)

100.   That feeling when you are about to land in Scotland is unmatched — the moment your plane breaks through the clouds and you catch your first glimpse of the landscape.

101. And finally, some Scottish words are just really fun to say.

clishmaclaver	Incessant chatter or gossip
eeksie-peeksie	Fair and equal to both sides, even-steven
gaberlunzie	A beggar
hamesucken	An assault on a person in their own home.
mixter-maxter	A chaotic jumble of stuff
smeddum	Common sense and admirable resourcefulness
stammygaster	A shocking and unpleasant surprise
tapsalteerie	Upside-down
thunder-plump	A sudden rainstorm with thunder
whigmaleerie	A decoration

7

scotland through the seasons

"There are two seasons in Scotland. June and Winter."
- Billy Connolly

The saying goes, "If you don't like the weather in Scotland, wait half an hour." In New England, where I live, there are (at least) four seasons. Scotland, on the other hand, is a place where the *days* have seasons.

You might have a warmish sunny morning and dress accordingly, only to have clouds roll in bringing cold, drenching rain… which might then give way to hailstones. Then, just as you think the day is a write off, the clouds break apart and it's back to warmish and sunny again… that is, until a chilly wind picks up, ushering in a dense fog. Wash, rinse, repeat. Forever.

The climate in Scotland may never be constant, but it's never extreme either. Therefore, any weather that is slightly out of the ordinary makes front page headlines and seems to put everyone in a mild state of panic.

Three days of 25°C (77°F) temperatures is declared a heatwave. (In other words, a Scottish "heatwave" is what everyone else calls nice summer weather.)

Likewise, a centimeter of snow will single handedly shut public services down and cause delays and endless aggravation. It's an amusing thing to witness as a New Englander who is used to sweltering 90 degree summers and back-to-back ten foot snowstorms in winter.

Because the seasons sort of blend together endlessly, they are punctuated by the celebrations and public holidays dotted throughout. This chapter gives you a short and sweet summary of what you might encounter over the course of an entire year in Scotland.

Spring

Flowers blooming in March

Spring in Scotland beats Spring in New England, I can tell you that right now. It's mild, the grass is greener than green, and there are flowers blooming everywhere as early as March. (The best we can hope for here that early in the year is slush and mud.) It does rain a lot though, which shouldn't surprise anyone at this point in the book. But... they have flowers!

MOTHER'S DAY

This one gets my husband in trouble every year: Mother's Day in Scotland is not in May. It's in March or early April. You can't really blame him for forgetting his poor mum back home because there are obviously no Mother's Day cards out yet here in the US. (Father's Day, however, is the same day for both countries, so he has no excuse with that one.)

EASTER

For kids, Easter in Scotland is not just about chocolate eggs, but *the* chocolate egg. Instead of an Easter basket delivered by the elusive Easter Bunny, everyone gets a giant hollow chocolate egg with more chocolates inside.

An Easter egg in Scotland. As you can see, they are not messing around over there.

And "egg" is a very loose definition: it can be pig shape, lamb shape, castle shape, Thomas the train shape. There's no fake grass or jelly beans (or Easter Bunny for that matter). Easter is all about the *chocolate*.

There may be an egg hunt in the back gairden, and there's usually something like a roast dinner. But the best part of Easter for most people (besides the chocolate) is Easter Holidays, which means a week or more off work and school.

Summer

A "summer's day" in Glasgow

True Summer weather doesn't really kick off in Scotland until June, when it's consistently mild for the next few months. I'd be lying if I said Summer in Scotland is all sunshine and warmth, but it's a definite improvement.

On the rare occasion when the the sun makes a prolonged appearance and the mercury rises above a certain degree, it becomes what is known as *taps aff* weather in Glasgow. This means that men everywhere will opt to go topless in unison, regardless of fitness or flabbiness.

When the air gets warm and muggy, it's described as *close*. But Scots don't have any cooling system in their houses. Window fans and central air conditioning are nonexistent because uncomfortably hot weather is never a problem for long. In fact, many summer days will still be *a bit fresh* (cool enough to actually shut the windows.)

But the biggest bonus about this time of year is the fact that the days go on *forever*. It stays light until almost midnight. In fact, up in the more northern reaches, they have the *simmer dim*, a time in midsummer when dusk runs directly into dawn because the sun never sets. For all the grimness that enshrouds most of the rest of the year, Scotland really redeems itself with this one.

If you're lucky enough to be in Scotland in the summer, I do have one tip for you: leave your shorts at home. I can't stress this enough. I promise you won't miss them. Your legs will freeze if the weather changes, which it will. You can get away with long jeans or trousers and a t-shirt all summer long and be perfectly comfortable. (But always bring a jacket, just to be safe.) Nobody wears flip-flops either. Those are strictly for the beach.

In Glasgow, the second half of July is known as *The Fair*, but it has nothing to do with an actual carnival anymore. (It did once, a long time ago.) It's the annual summer holiday where many businesses close down, and for two weeks everyone from office workers to builders get at least some of that time off work. In other parts of Scotland, it's known as *The Trades*, and it can be a fortnight in either July or August depending on location.

Autumn

First of all, it's "Autumn", never "Fall", in Scotland. If you come from a part of the US with beautiful autumns, you might find yourself a bit more homesick than usual during this season if you're staying in Scotland long term. Nothing compares to Fall in New England. Instead of crisp air and leaves in brilliant hues under blue skies, in Scotland, it just gets soggier and soggier and darker and darker. (Autumn is also the rainiest season in an already rainy country.) There's no apple picking, hayrides, or cider donuts.

And now that I've mentioned cider, I have to point out that in the UK, cider is *always* hard cider. If you ask for cider, you're never going to get that tangy, opaque apple juice that we associate with Fall. It doesn't exist in that innocent form. They usually have it on drought right alongside beer at pubs, so you can ask for a pint of cider (it's about the same alcohol content as beer). The cheaper varieties come in garish colors like electric blue, and are a favorite of both teenagers and down-and-outs.

Oh, and you're not going to find pumpkin spice anything, except for rare American novelty items. You might find pumpkins in some supermarkets, but they're also more of a novelty. Needless to say, pumpkin pie is also nonexistent. (However, you'll probably find it amusing how easily you can get a Scot hooked on it if you can get them to try it.) Even cinnamon is surprisingly hard to find. You might actually be surprised to learn that our national obsession with putting cinnamon in cereal and anything sweet is seen as very weird outside the US.

We Americans go all out decorating for Autumn, with our pumpkins and gourds, scarecrows, cornstalks and other countrified harvest-themed fall decor. You'll rarely find any of this in Scotland. Autumn is just a stopgap between summer and Christmas, without the existence of Thanksgiving to mark the season. (However, the concept of Black Friday is unfortunately spreading.)

HALLOWEEN

Halloween is not nearly as big a deal as it is in the US, although we can thank pagan Scotland for its entire existence. (Halloween actually comes from the Scottish word *Allhallow-even*.) You won't see a pumpkin on every doorstep because, like I said, pumpkins aren't really a thing (and they would probably get smashed within a day, just for being so out of the ordinary.

There's an old tradition called *guisin'* where children would put on disguises and go door-to-door singing and telling jokes in exchange for nuts, fruit or sweets, which was an early form of trick-or-treating. Nowadays, if children trick-or-treat at all, it's mostly at family and friend's houses, and they might get loose change in addition to candy.

But, just like most things, American-style Halloween is creeping across the Atlantic and it seems to get bigger and bigger in Scotland every year.

GUY FAWKES NIGHT

"Remember, Remember the 5th of November", as the saying goes. And remember it you shall, when you hear fireworks exploding in every direction. We have 4th of July

for our fireworks; the UK has the 5th of November (Guy Fawkes Night, or Bonfire Night). The big difference is people in the UK create their own individual firework displays. And with houses and gairdens so close together, it can get quite… dramatic. Fireworks are legal and readily available, and even children find a way to get ahold of them. So, yeah. Your best bet is really just to enjoy the excitement from your window when this festive firework season approaches.

ST ANDREW'S DAY

The patron saint of Scotland gets his own day on the 30th of November every year, but sadly for him, it is largely ignored. (St. Patrick gets all the love.)

Winter

Winter is a not-so-subtle reminder that Scotland is the most northern part of an island that is already quite far north, right up there with Scandinavia. So when the nights start **drawing in** during the winter months, that means the sun starts setting in the middle of the afternoon. (We're talking as early as 3pm.) This can be depressing, to say the least.

A frosty afternoon sunset in December.

Not only that, it's cold. As someone who grew up with extreme New England winters where the bottom falls out of the thermometer, you'd think I'd be used to cold. But there's cold, and then there's Scottish Cold. (The Scots have a word for it — *baltic*.) This is the kind of damp cold that seeps through jackets straight into your bones. My aunt told me never in her life has she felt colder than she did when she visited Edinburgh in January.

A frosted Lacoste.

The thing is, it's rarely below freezing. So why is it so baltic? The wind, for a start. Scotland is a very windy country, as I mentioned earlier. Another huge factor is high humidity, which throws off your body's temperature regulation *and* really does seep into your clothes. For this reason, insulated, water resistant coats are preferable to fleece or down puffer coats in cold weather. Think protection rather than fluffiness. (And layers. Lots of layers.) As the saying goes, "there's no such thing as bad weather, only the wrong clothes."

So, just to recap: it's exceptionally dark, baltic, and things shut down without warning. Needless to say, Winter is not the easiest season to be in Scotland. Thankfully though, there is plenty of celebrating to get you through it.

CHRISTMAS

The Christmas season in Scotland might as well be called the *Pished*-mas season, because if you think the Scots drink a lot during the year, just you wait until December. It's a time of year when you can watch celebrity chefs get visibly drunk as they prepare their Christmas dishes on TV. (Celebrity chefs get drunk year round. Well, some do.)

But in spite of all this merriment, Christmas is above all the time of year to **coorie in** (get nestled and snuggle up) and enjoy being home with family, putting the fire on and watching all the Christmas specials of your favorite shows on TV. It's the quintessential holiday for homebodies, which most Scots secretly are.

Many Scots, including children, get a full two weeks off work and school for Christmas and the day after Christmas (Boxing Day), which is a bonus public holiday for everyone.

Here's a breakdown of what you can probably expect at Christmastime in Scotland:

- You'll notice the Scots will add *"yer"* (your) before Christmas. So they might ask a child, *"What do you want for yer Christmas?"*
- "Happy Christmas" is said much more frequently than "Merry Christmas".
- Fresh trees are a lot less common than artificial ones, but they are available. You won't, however, find nearly as many wreaths on front doors.
- The Scots go just as decor-happy as we do, with the blinking lights and giant blow-up Santas and whatnot. (By the way, Christmas lights are called fairy lights.)
- Some shops start putting up Christmas decorations in October (though this isn't unheard of Stateside either.)
- Christmas crackers are wrapped paper tubes that two people pop apart (it makes a loud noise) and out fly cheap toys, fortune-cookie-like jokes, and paper crowns. Then people of all ages wear said paper crowns at Christmas dinner.
- Advent calendars with each door revealing a piece of chocolate for every day in December, are another tradition.
- Christmas cards are often displayed stringed up along the wall, rather than just the mantle. (And there seems to be a proliferation of teddy bears on Christmas cards.)

- *Buck's fizz* (champagne and orange juice — basically, a mimosa) is traditionally served with breakfast on Christmas morning.
- One thing that surprised me is that eggnog is not really a thing. In fact, most Scots probably just know of it from American movies, and it might even sound weird to them. Egg as a mixer actually does sound strange if you think about it. In New England, egg nog is so important it makes its first appearance alongside the milk by October. The closest equivalent you'll find in Scotland is advocaat in the liqueur section. It tastes weirdly similar.
- The big meal on Christmas day closely resembles what we Americans eat on Thanksgiving. The customary Christmas Dinner is a big roast turkey served with roast potatoes, stuffing, some type of vegetable (like brussels sprouts or carrots), all drenched in a big pool of brown gravy. (The Scots love drenching things in gravy. Nothing is safe.) There might be additional special side dishes like mini sausages or rolled-up bacon.
- The dessert is usually individual mince pies (despite the name, this is the one time pies *don't* have meat in them. Mince means minced dried fruit in this case.) It might also be a Christmas pudding, which is essentially a boozy fruit cake. Other sweets like shortbread, tablet and chocolate (lots of chocolate!) will also make a much-appreciated appearance.
- Instead of leaving out cookies and milk, Santa gets mince pies and sherry, with a carrot for Rudolph.

HOGMANAY

If you think Christmas is a big deal, you ain't seen nothin' yet. Hogmanay (New Year's Eve) is *huge* in Scotland. It is the most important holiday of the year (for adults, anyway). There's actually a reason for this: Christmas was banned for hundreds of years because it was seen as too "Catholic" by the Protestant Referendum, and treated as just a regular workday. Believe it or not, Christmas wasn't even a public holiday in Scotland until 1958. So, Hogmanay took its place as the main winter holiday to eat, drink and be merry with loved ones, and that mindset has kind of stuck ever since.

The place to be as a visitor in Scotland for New Years is definitely Edinburgh. They have pipes, live music and concerts, a street party, and of course fireworks, with the castle (atop its extinct volcano) providing the majestic backdrop. But my own personal favorite place to be is at a house party with family and friends at home, with good food and plenty of bevvy. (Many people would agree that this is the very best way to celebrate it.)

This Hogmanay house party has only just begun.

Hogmanay specials of Scottish TV shows will play back to back, as well *Hogmanay Live*, hosted by Jackie Bird. There's lots of singing, both on TV and off. Those who can play instruments usually do. Then, as midnight approaches, the broadcast switches to Edinburgh castle, and the countdown begins.

The moment the clock strikes twelve is known as **The Bells**, and if you thought you were already partying before, you'll find you were wrong. The party's actually just beginning now. Everyone crosses their arms and links hands and forms a circle, singing **Auld Lang Syne**. Then everyone goes around the room, kissing cheeks, drunken "Happy New Year"s are exchanged, drams are poured, champagne popped, and the celebration continues well into the wee hours. The excitement is infectious and you can see why it's the most anticipated holiday of the year.

One of the traditions of Hogmanay is **First Footing**. Whoever the very first person is to set foot in your house in the new year is your **First Foot**. For good luck, it should be a tall, dark and handsome man. (Redheads and blonds are unlucky, having something to do with fair-haired Viking invaders.) Your First Foot should also bear a gift, traditionally a coin (representing prosperity), shortbread (food), coal (warmth), or whisky (good cheer). **Black bun**, a pastry-wrapped dark fruitcake, is also a traditional Hogmanay treat, which might also be brought as a gift by First Footers. And nobody should cross the threshold before the First Foot, either in or out.

In Scotland, Hogmanay is so important that both the first *and* the second of January are public holidays. That added day of recovery, you'll discover, is a definite bonus.

BURNS NIGHT

The 25th of January is Burns Night, the annual celebration of Scotland's national poet, Robert Burns, also known as "The Bard". A Burns Supper is eaten that night, which includes haggis, *neeps and tatties* (turnips and mashed potatoes). Traditionally someone will recite Burns' poem, "An Ode to a Haggis" before eating, and there will be numerous whisky-fueled toasts in his honor. (Any excuse, right?)

***

IF YOU'LL BE SPENDING A YEAR (OR MORE) IN SCOTLAND...

Remember that Scots will make any excuse to celebrate. You can take comfort in the fact that no matter where you are in the year, no matter how bad the weather gets or how infrequently you see that shiny yellow disk in the sky, there's always another celebration around the corner. (And if you've *really* had it, Spain is just a short flight away.)

8

make yerself at hame

PICTURE A HOUSE in Scotland, and you might envision a stone cottage nestled on a misty moor speckled with cloud-white sheep, with craggy mountains providing a majestic backdrop. That's the dream... but very few people actually live like that.

*Contrary to popular belief, this is **not** a typical Scottish house.*

So, what's the average house actually like in Scotland? Well, first of all, although Scotland is a very old country with some *very* old buildings, most people don't actually live in old houses. Quite the opposite. Most people live in houses that are several decades old tops, unless they've paid a pretty penny. Here in New England, I've always lived in houses built in the 1700s and 1800s, and haven't thought twice about it. While that might not be considered "old" by Scottish standards, it's surprisingly uncommon for someone to actually *live* in a house that old.

There aren't many standalone private homes with spacious yards in Scotland either. Neighborhoods are dense, and people tend to live in very close proximity to their neighbors. Most houses are attached terrace houses (or rowhouses) grouped together in villages, or neighborhoods of linking roads where every block of housing is a similar style. You'll also see semi-detached (duplexes) or bungalows (detached single story houses). Even if you do have a detached house with no shared walls with neighbors, your backyard (or **back gairden**) will usually run up against your neighbors' all sides, separated by fences or rows of shrubbery. This means back gairdens are enclosed, which parents of young children and pets appreciate.

People also live on a much smaller scale. The average **hoose** (house) in Scotland is not just kind of small, it is tiny. (You'll hear the word "shoebox" thrown around a lot to describe the size of houses.) The average house size in the UK is about 800 square feet, so houses considered small in the US still feel luxuriously spacious compared to Scottish houses.

With so little space, unfortunately storage is also in short supply. Closets are a rarity, and you won't always find one in every bedroom either. The most storage you'll get in any given house is the loft, or attic (which is more like a crawl space), because basements aren't a thing either.

VILLAGE LIFE

Many people on the outskirts of Scottish cities and towns live in housing estates, or villages. One type of village is called a housing scheme. A housing scheme, or just "scheme", is a village made up of council houses. These houses are built by the local government to be rented out at an affordable rate, with the option of buying. The tradeoff is that there is a waiting list, and you have no choice which neighborhood or house you're placed in (or who your neighbors will be). Some schemes have a bad reputation because anyone from any situation can be placed there, and it takes very few bad apples to spoil the bunch.

Whether it's a housing scheme or private development, most every village has at least one *corner shop* (convenience store) and a local pub. Many have hair salons, restaurants, post offices, butchers, bakers, small businesses, takeaway places, betting shops, etc. that directly serve the local population. There's a reason housing estates are known as villages… because they really are.

Council houses in a typical Scottish housing scheme.

A local fishmonger van arrives for whoever wants fish or other groceries. Some villages have mobile libraries. And no matter what season it is, you'll hear chiming music and that means the *icey* (ice cream van) is nearby. The icey sells more than just ice cream — often they have crisps, sweets, bread or even cigarettes.

The fishmonger delivering fish and fresh groceries in a village.

Up until relatively recently, everyone still had milk delivered on their doorstep in glass bottles by the milkman. The empty bottles would be put back out and replaced with fresh ones every morning. When my husband was a kid, after a night of camping, he and his friends would run up to a random neighbor's doorstep and nick a freshly delivered cold bottle of milk to drink for breakfast.

Almost every village also has its own post office. (One interesting thing to note: mail is called *post* in the UK, but they have The Royal Mail. We call it mail, but we have the United States Post Office.) The postal delivery worker is called the *postie*. Instead of individual mailboxes, everyone has a slot in their front door which the post is dropped through. If something doesn't fit through, you receive a notice that you have a parcel waiting for you to pick up at the post office. And the postie never picks outgoing mail up at your door either, but you can drop it in the nearest postbox.

YER WEE HOOSIE

You won't see any wooden houses in Scotland. That's an American thing. Scottish houses have either brick, stone or roughcast exteriors (roughcasting is a plaster of lime, shells, and pebbles, originally invented to cover poor quality brickwork.) Because of this, they're very sturdy and resistant to the constant wet weather. (Unlike wood.)

If you live in a terraced house, the *close* (rhymes with "dose") is the passageway that leads off the main street to back gairdens. Without the close, there would be no easy way, for example, to bring your *wheelie bins* (trash cans) from the back of your house to the curb on trash day for the *bin lorry* (garbage truck) to pick up.

Most back gairdens will have a gairden shed, which not only serves as extra storage space, but also a substitute basement, garage and workshop (few Scottish houses have any of these.) The gairden shed is a stereotypically masculine space for that reason — a man cave in miniature.

If they want more space, some people add *conservatories* to the back of their houses, which are similar to what we call sunrooms. They're well-lit spaces with lots of windows and skylights, usable year round, regardless of the weather outside (which, let's face it, is unpredictable at best).

One interesting thing I have seen in some Scottish houses is that some front doors lock with a key from the *inside*. So you need a key to lock yourself in, and let yourself out again. The windows are the same, some with actual locks on them that you need a key for. (Good luck if you can't reach that key in a fire!) Apparently there is a law in Scotland that stealing from a place secured by a lock (*lockfast*) is a more serious offense than stealing from an unlocked place, which might partially explain this.

Windows open inward or outward with a handle, rather than sliding up and down as they do in American houses. You'll also notice that there are *no screens* on windows in Scotland. This is simply because there aren't nearly as many bugs that want to get inside. (No mosquitos!) Sure, you get the occasional house fly, or maybe a moth at night, but they're just seen as minor annoyances.

Scottish houses have more interior doors than American houses. They will often even have a door from the front doorway to the main living area. This is probably because houses used to be drafty before central heating became standard, not too long ago. Our overgrown American houses tend to be more open-plan — we have an unhealthy obsession with removing doors and knocking out walls when we remodel.

TAKE THE HEAT

Scottish houses are heated with gas, never oil. You'll usually find radiators in every room, flush against the wall, which kick off a surprising amount of heat. Although houses aren't as drafty as they used to be before double-glazing and central heating, most still have a fireplace in the living room for added coziness. Chances are good, however, you'll never encounter a real wood one. Most fireplaces are gas, turned on with the flip of a switch, with artificial coals. As with just about everything else, they're much more scaled down in size than a typical American fireplace.

FEEL THE POWER

Using electricity in the UK requires a little more attention to detail than you're used to. Look at any outlet on the wall, and, apart from general differences in the socket shape, you'll notice that they all have an on/off switch. When you plug something in, you must also make sure the outlet switch is flipped *on*, or you'll be scratching your head wondering why it isn't working. And, when you are finished with whatever you're using — especially if you want to unplug it — you should then flip the outlet switch off.

These switched outlets are much safer than having live, open outlets everywhere, and for good reason: electricity in the UK is 240 volts, double what we are used to Stateside (120 volts). That's twice as dangerous and twice as deadly. An electric shock in the UK can literally send you flying across the room. (However, thanks to a variety of other built-in safety measures which I won't pretend to be an expert on, the UK electrical system makes ours seem "shockingly" primitive in comparison.)

Now that we've covered the basics, let's go on a house tour, shall we?

POTTERING ABOUT IN THE KITCHEN

My mother-in-law, like many Scots, sometimes calls her kitchen the old-fashioned word *scullery*.

And once you set foot in a Scottish scullery, the first thing you'll find on the countertop is something that is a permanent fixture in every household: the electric kettle. This kettle has a flip switch that will boil water in about a minute. Once you've experienced this, you can never go back to stovetop kettles. There are many uses for the electric kettle, like quickly boiling water for pasta,

I get so hot for you

but its primary purpose is for making tea. And lots of it. (We've already covered just how much Scottish people like tea.) Electric kettles can be purchased in the US too, and we use ours everyday. But we've noticed it doesn't boil anywhere near as fast, due to the difference in voltage. (That's probably why they haven't caught on here.)

Near the kettle is the sink, and the water that comes out of that tap is not only drinkable, but it is the best tap water I've ever tasted, making it easy to stay well-hydrated. And, because it's soft water, not hard water (it has fewer mineral deposits that leave behind a residue), it's better for washing your hair, and everything else, too. Fun fact: water in Scotland is not metered, so you can technically use as much as you want without the consequences of a hefty water bill. (However, that's not a license to waste water. Not that you would, anyway.)

Washing up means the act of doing the dishes, so you can probably hazard a guess that *washing up liquid* is dish soap. Because dishwashers aren't standard in every home, the washing up is sometimes done by hand. There's a bizarre stereotype that British people don't bother to rinse their dishes, leaving them to dry with soap bubbles on them and everything. It must be an English thing though, since I've never witnessed this in Scotland. One thing you *won't* normally find in the sink is a garbage disposal, so food waste goes right in the *bin* (trash).

Moving on from the sink to kitchen appliances. Let's start with the fridge. Like all things in Scotland, it's likely going to be... more compact. Don't expect to be able to stuff a week's worth of groceries into the refrigerator: a standard Scottish fridge-freezer is about as spacious as two dorm fridges stacked on top of each other. (That's if you're lucky. Sometimes it's just the size of one dorm fridge that fits under the counter.) You'll find that because of this, even the containers that food comes in are smaller. (I've never seen a big fat gallon-sized jug of milk in Scotland.) Consequently, you will *also* run out of things more frequently. You just have to follow the European method of shopping for fresh groceries as you need them, rather than all at once.

The large appliance used for cooking food is called the **cooker** (the stove), and if you have a gas cooker, as most people do, you're in for another adjustment. The temperature is measured not by degrees, but by **gas marks**. Recipes will also often state that a dish should be placed in a cool, moderate or hot oven. Generally, a warm oven is Gas mark 3; a moderate oven, gas mark 4; a somewhat hot oven, gas marks 5 - 6; a hot oven, gas mark 7; and a very hot oven is gas marks 8 - 9.

THE NEVERENDING JOY OF LAUNDRY

You can forget about a laundry room. Unless you're very lucky, the washer and dryer are often right there in the kitchen too. (They are therefore honorary kitchen appliances.) Again, they are microscopic by American standards, so not only do you have to food shop more frequently, you have to do laundry more frequently too. This is not so bad when it's just an adult or two, but when you have kids, the constant laundry gets a little overwhelming.

While my mother-in-law was raising her four kids, she had actual washing lines on a pulley system strung up on her kitchen ceiling. The process of doing laundry must have lasted 30 years straight for her. And yet, being the lovely woman she is, she still insists on doing ours and handing it to us in neatly folded piles when we're visiting. I'm grateful for this, at the very least because I wouldn't be able to figure her washing machine out anyway. Every British washing machine I've come across has been extremely over-complicated, with multiple knobs, buttons and cryptic numbers and symbols.

Surprise: even laundry detergent is different. There are two different kinds to acquaint yourself with: biological or nonbiological. **Bio** contains enzymes that break down stains easily and work in lower temperatures (30-50°C). **Non-bio** is preferable if you have sensitive skin, but it requires a higher temperature to be as effective. Liquid laundry detergent is not as popular as tablets.

Okay, so now that we've washed our clothes, it's time to dry them. It might seem counterintuitive in such a wet country, but tumble dryers are not seen as standard appliances and many homes don't have them. But, if they do, there are two different kinds. There's the American-style vented dryer, with a hose vent that goes out the nearest open window. Or there's the condenser dryer (sometimes a washer/dryer combo), which doesn't require a vent, and instead captures the water in a container which needs to be emptied.

I've experienced both, and they each have their pros and cons. The American-style dries clothes faster, but it needs to be near a window, and you'll be freezing on a cold day with the window open. The condenser dryer can be put anywhere in the house, and warms the house up so well that you can forgo central heating altogether, but it takes much, much longer to do the job (and that extra heat might not be so appreciated on already warm days.)

You'll see clotheslines in constant use out in people's back gairdens, whether or not they have a tumble dryer. Again, counterintuitive for a rainy climate, but I guess it frees up space inside (those tiny dryers don't fit much anyway), it saves on energy costs, and clothes smell nice when they dry in the breeze. If/when it rains, everything is brought in and dried on drying racks near radiators. Since I've lived in Scotland, I'm still in the habit of rack drying my favorite clothes and jeans. Although my industrial-sized American dryer has its perks, I think air drying keeps my clothes looking newer longer, and they hold their shape better

DOWN THE TOILET
When we say toilet in America, we're obviously talking about that porcelain bowl where sh*t happens. Literally. The Scots, on the other hand, call their entire bathroom **the toilet**. So when you need to go, you say *"I need the toilet."* And if you really, really need to go, you say

you're *"burstin'"* and everyone knows what you mean and will promptly get out of your way.

You could also call the toilet the **bog**, but if you want to go full on Scottish, call it the **lavvy** or the **cludgie**. Toilet paper is **toilet roll** or **bog roll**.

Most houses have only one toilet, and it's frequently at the top of the stairs. And the actual toilet itself? The first thing you'll notice is that the water level is much lower. Then, when you eventually flush, you'll notice some some impressive (and noisy) flush power. Toilets are just much more... shall we say, efficient over there. Let's just say you have to work really hard at clogging a Scottish toilet.

In older houses, you might also experience the uniquely British phenomenon of non-mixer taps. One tap comes out skin-meltingly hot, and the other comes out ice cold. Apparently you're either meant to wash your hands quickly under the cold tap, or plug the drain and fill the basin to create a tolerable temperature. The two taps thing is a hangover from old building codes: the cold water had to be potable, the hot did not.

Not every toilet has a medicine cabinet, or even a mirror, and you'll frequently see everything lined up on little shelves. But one thing you'll *never* find in the toilet (it still feels funny saying that) is outlets, or even light switches. It would violate the UK's strict Health and Safety codes.

Having said that, you might come face to face with an **electric shower**. Those two words *really* don't sound like they should go together, but bear with me here. Basically, an electric shower is a wall unit attached to a showerhead that heats the water immediately before it's dispensed. The hot water comes out with the touch of a button instead of the turn of a faucet. It's more economical than relying on the boiler to keep a large quantity of shower water hot at all times. Talk about irony though: Outlets are strictly forbidden in bathrooms, but electric showers are a-okay.

NIGHT NIGHT

The Scots call their bed their *scratcher*. Does this originate from the days when every bed had bedbugs? I'm guessing so. But the word is still very much in use today.

The words for bed sizes are slightly different. What we call a twin bed is a **single bed**, an American Queen size is a UK King, and an American King size is a Super King.

While we like a big puffy comforter to snuggle up under, they love a good duvet (doo-vay) over there. Basically, a duvet is like a thin, plain comforter that you tuck inside a duvet cover, like a pillow in a pillowcase. Because the cover is an extra thin layer of fabric, there's no need for a flat sheet, which are hard to find anyway. It makes more sense for tiny washing machines because you can remove and wash only the cover as needed. You can also change up the look of the whole bedroom easily with a new duvet cover, instead of buying all new bedding. The annoying part is actually figuring out how to get the duvet to lie flat and evenly inside the duvet cover. I have yet to crack that one.

A lot of houses don't have closets in the bedrooms. (Where I live in the US, bedrooms without closets wouldn't even be considered legal bedrooms at all.) Instead, people buy *wardrobes*, which are tall cabinets with a rack to hang clothes and a few additional compartments for storage.

A few more house terms to know...

Cooker	Oven
Grill	Broiler
Hame	Home
Hoose	House
Kitchen roll	Paper towels
Leccy	Slang for your electricity and associated bills
Press	Pantry
Redd up	To tidy your house
Scullery	Kitchen
Skirting board	Baseboards
Tea towel	A thin dishcloth
Up the stair (*always singular*)	Upstairs

9

take the high road: getting around in scotland

A bus shelter in a Scottish village.

DRIVING

One great thing about Scotland is because it's a fairly small country, pretty much everything is within driving distance.

And yes, thankfully, you *can* legally drive with your American license. But only for a year. After that, you must obtain a Scottish license. That means passing a road test, theory test and everything. A word of warning: even if you're an experienced driver with a perfect record, passing the UK driving test on your first try is no picnic, according to Americans who have done it.

You'll also quickly discover that most cars are still manual transmission in the UK, which they actually seem to prefer over there. (I've heard automatics dismissively referred to as "go carts" a few times.)

If you pass your driving test in an automatic, you are also not authorized to drive a manual. The reverse is *not* true. (By the way, nobody calls it stick shift.) When you're learning to drive in Scotland, you must display a red "L" plate. When you see an L in the rear window of someone's car, you know they're a "learner" and new to driving.

Your car is called your **motor** or **brief**. And, like just about everything else, cars are smaller. You'll see the brand names you're familiar with, but they're scaled down versions that often look unrecognizable. You'll regularly see models of cars you never knew existed, and car brands you might have hardly encountered at all in the US: Vauxhall, Peugeot, Renault, Citroën, Fiat etc. While SUVs are gaining popularity, they're still noticeably less roomy than their American counterparts.

Just like the rest of the UK, they drive on the *left* in Scotland. Therefore, everything is in reverse. The steering wheel is on the right so the radio and everything else is to your left. (Thankfully the pedals are in the same position, or we'd all be screwed.) The fact everything is mirror-imaged actually makes it easier for your brain to adjust to driving on the opposite side of the road. However, old habits die hard, and you might catch yourself going to the door on the wrong side of the car longer than you'd probably want to admit.

Remember also that the slow lane on the *motorway* (highway/freeway) is on the left, and you always pass on the right.

Streets are also narrower. Yet at the same time, it feels like people drive much faster on them than most Americans would feel comfortable on the same width of street. What makes this even more illogical is that many two-way streets have only enough space for one car at a time, so drivers often have to stop and pull over (and sometimes even back up) to let another car get by. It becomes a nightmare when there are also cars parallel parked on that same street. (I'm wincing just thinking about that scenario.)

A lot of cars (yes, cars) are also diesel powered. Apparently diesel offers better mileage than *petrol* (gasoline), which is ridiculously expensive in Europe, and therefore more economical over there.

The roads are generally curvier and less grid-like. Instead of intersections every few blocks, there are *roundabouts*. In the US we call them traffic circles, and contrary to popular belief, we actually *do* have them here, where I live at least, but they are vanishingly rare. (Not that anyone here actually knows what to do on them anyway.) Because everything is in reverse, the traffic flow is clockwise, as opposed to counterclockwise. So, when entering one, look and give way to the right.

Sometimes there are even mini roundabouts that look like big buttons in the middle of the road. The purpose of these is simply to force traffic to slow down.

Because of all these roundabouts, you'll find that driving is a lot less start-and-stop in general (which makes sense if most cars are manual).

Traffic lights look about the same, apart from the fact that yellow is called *amber*. The only difference is, when a red light is about to turn green, the traffic light displays red and amber simultaneously to warn you. And "right on red" isn't a thing, so don't even try it!

A few more driving terms to know...

Bonnet	Hood
Boot	Trunk
Car park	Parking lot
Caravan	Camper trailer
Dual carriageway	Divided highway
Estate car	Station wagon
Flyover	Overpass
Jumpleads	Jumper cables
Number plate	License plate
People carrier	Passenger van/minivan
Road-works	Construction, roadwork

Saloon	Four-door car (sedan)
Sleeping policeman	Speedbump
Slip road	A short road used to get on or off a major road
Turn-indicators	Turn signals
Windscreen	Windshield
Wing mirrors	Side mirrors

Now, having said all this, you might not actually need to drive *at all*. Scotland is nowhere near as car-centric as we are. This is because not only is petrol shockingly expensive, but public transport options are first-class (as much as you'll hear people complain about them). Because of this, many people never bother getting their license at all, with no stigma attached. Which brings me to my next point...

PUBLIC TRANSPORT

You can pretty much take a train or bus to any corner of not only Scotland, but the entire UK. You can just as easily get into the city centre as you can get way out to the countryside. Unless you're way out in the farthest reaches of the most remote island, there will be service wherever you live, usually either a bus or train stop or both (even if you sometimes have to walk a bit. But you'll become very used to walking). And everything links up.

Commuters on a typical double decker bus.

If you don't feel like waiting on a schedule, taxis are just a phone call away too. You're never stranded without a car like you would be here. Taxis are usually available immediately when called. You don't need to arrange them ahead of time. The only time you might be waiting for a while is during peak late night weekend hours. If you're actually out in "the toun", however, there are *taxi stances* everywhere, where black cabs (like in London) are always lining up waiting for their next customer.

Trains (Scotrail) are modern and futuristic, and they glide quietly along the tracks. If you're wondering why I'm saying this, when I used to board the commuter rail to Boston to go to work, I had to cover my ears so I wouldn't be deafened by the engine noise and the screeching brakes of the 40 year old trains — which still had their original 1970s groovy wood panelling inside.

The interior of this typical Scottish commuter train looks downright futuristic compared to some of the American ones I've been on.

By the way, don't be surprised to see people in full business attire uncorking a bottle of wine on trains in the middle of the day. Some of the longer distance trains actually have drinks trolleys that come around. Yes, trains in Scotland are glorified mobile pubs too. I guess that's a testament to how... pleasant they are?

You can buy your ticket on board when the ticket collector passes, but you can also buy it ahead of time online, or at the station. And don't make the mistake of losing your ticket either (like I might), because you'll also need it when you arrive at the station for inspection or at the turnstiles.

GETTING ON YOUR FEET

Despite being spoiled for choice with modes of transport, you'll probably find yourself walking a lot more than you usually do no matter what. Places tend to be designed for walkability, not necessarily drivability so make sure you *really* like your shoes, no joke.

Scotland has sidewalks everywhere so it's very safe for pedestrians — unless that is, you plan to step off the sidewalk. This is where things get dicey. If you want to cross the street, first of all, make sure you're actually *looking the right way* before your foot leaves the curb. This could mean the difference between life and death, seriously. I say this not  only because traffic is coming at you in the opposite direction, but because everyone drives *insanely* fast. And unlike the US, nobody expects pedestrians to ever be in the road apart from at crosswalks.

Zebra crossings are the only crosswalks, apart from the ones with actual traffic lights, where pedestrians always have the right of way. They are easily recognized by the black and white stripes painted across the road.

10

street smarts, scottish style

HOW TO DRESS

If you've never been to Scotland before, you might picture the soggy climate and rugged landscape, and all the walking I've been warning you about on those hilly city streets — and pack for practicality: performance hiking shoes, cozy hooded sweatshirts, shapeless windbreakers, etc. But I can assure you if you put function before form too much, you are going to feel underdressed and frumpy, unless you are literally spending your entire visit camping on a moor. (In that case I envy you, but never mind.)

Scotland, like anywhere in Europe, is just not as casual as most of us are Stateside. Let's just face it: we Americans as a whole are some of the most casual dressers on earth, and tend to put comfort above all else. If we put any extra effort in our appearance without a compelling reason, we'll be asked what the occasion is. We wear PJs in public, for chrissake. That's something you really can't get away with outside of North America.

Women in Scotland tend to enjoy getting dolled up: hair and nails, makeup and eyebrows "on point", false eyelashes, accessorizing, the works. Men, too, care about their appearance, with styled hair, fitted clothing, nice shoes, shirt collars, and aftershave. Of course, there are exceptions which you'll no doubt encounter. But what I'm trying to say is, don't be afraid to put a bit of extra effort in.

If your aim is to avoid looking like a tourist, lean more toward dressing up rather than dressing down — and you'll blend in just fine.

What to wear in Scotland:

- Layers, layers, and more layers of lightweight clothing
- Comfortable (but stylish) shoes or boots
- Wedge or thick heels (if you must wear stilettos, always carry flats to change into)
- Stylish sneakers/trainers (not gym or running shoes)
- Scarves
- Fitted and tailored, rather than relaxed and baggy (both men and women!)
- Skinny jeans/trousers, rather than loose or flare (both men and women!)
- Darker and neutral colors
- A water resistant but stylish jacket (like a trench coat or leather jacket), preferably with a hood!

What NOT to wear in Scotland:

- Shorts
- Shoes with exposed toes (due to puddles of rain, mud or anything else)
- Flip flops
- Bright, loud patterns and colors
- Baseball caps
- Baggy sweatshirts (or baggy anything)
- Big puffy down coats (you'll get soaked)
- Snow boots (never needed)
- Rain poncho or slicker (nobody wears these!)
- Pajamas or sweats in public (leggings are fine — on women)
- Kilts or tartan
- Anything associated with Celtic or Rangers!

Of course, these are only suggestions. If you genuinely don't care, you don't have to follow any of them (and more power to you).

HOW TO WALK DOWN THE STREET

This is a funny one, but many Americans in the UK have observed this quirky phenomenon: sometimes when you're walking down the sidewalk (or *pavement*, as they call it), it feels like other pedestrians will make a point to "play chicken" with you, even if you are staying in your lane. If you're not assertive, you'll always be the one who has to give way, and it can get annoying — because sometimes they will bump right into you if you don't.

So, how do you avoid a sidewalk zombie encounter like this? The trick is to stand your ground and look straight ahead to make it clear where you're intending to walk. And remember the traffic flow. People drive on the left, so they tend to walk on the left.

And remember to always say "sorry" if you need to get past someone. "Excuse me" implies *they're* in the wrong.

It's just a very slight language adjustment that makes all the difference.

HOW TO TAKE THE ESCALATOR

Always stand on the right and walk on the *left*. Most escalators even have a notice as you get on which says exactly this.

HOW TO QUEUE

It's an old cliche that still rings true: folks in Britain love to queue. (Yes, that rhyme was intentional.) They have elevated the act of lining up to an artform over there. The only thing you need to know about queuing is that you respect the queue. Never, ever "jump the queue" (cut in line). That is a cardinal sin in the UK. At a bus stop, for example, you board the bus in the exact order you arrived at the bus stop. There is no getting around this, it's how it's done.

HOW TO TIP

The Scots *do not* have a tipping culture. Unlike the US, they are paid a decent wage for their job and do not need to be tipped to make up the difference. This is especially true at pubs and restaurants — generally there is a service charge already tacked onto your bill. It is not necessary to pay the person twice. If you do choose to tip, make sure it's because you're actually impressed with the service, and not out of guilt or obligation. The standard American twenty percent would be borderline obscene — about ten percent is standard, but even that is not a fast rule. Many people let taxi drivers keep the change, for example.

THE BEAUTY OF V.A.T.

If you're confused by your newfound collection of unfamiliar banknotes and coins, at least you can count on the fact that the listed price of an item is in fact the actual price of the item. VAT (Value Added Tax) means the tax is already included in the item's cost, so there's no watching your total jump up at the register as it does Stateside. That means you can count out exactly what you owe ahead of time, instead of figuring it out at the checkout as a queue builds behind you. Or, you could just use your card.

USING YOUR CARD

You should be able to use your American bank card pretty much anywhere without issue (as long as your bank at home was informed that you're abroad so they don't freeze your account. Which, believe me, they will.) But you might have a bit of unexpected hassle if you still have a swipe card. Most cards in the UK are on the chip & pin system and have been for at least a decade, whereby you insert your card into a reader instead of swiping it. Because swipe cards are now so unusual, the cashier might not understand how to run the card and it might cause a holdup. (This has happened to me on a few occasions before my bank finally caught up with modern technology and issued me my own chip card.)

PUBLIC TOILETS

The Scots are seriously spoiled when it comes to public restrooms. The stalls go straight down to the floor! No half-inch gaps at the sides of the door either. You get actual privacy. More often than not, you even get your own private room within the restroom, with four walls around you and a real locking door. Yes, they actually trust you with a *real door*, folks.

Another thing you'll notice is that there are almost never paper towels. Air dryers are the norm. Also, due to the perpetually damp and windy weather, some nicer public restrooms have coin-operated hair straighteners, just in case your hair is having a "moment" (as mine often does in Scotland.)

Occasionally, you'll have to *spend a penny*, or use a pay toilet (for quite a bit more than a penny nowadays), but this is literally a small price to pay for the convenience.

CLOSING TIME?

Here's where we Americans are the spoiled ones: we know we can walk into most stores as late as 10 or 11 at night. Retail hours here in the USA are generally straightforward: we expect that most stores open early and close late. This is not the case in Scotland. Many businesses will shut at 5 or 6 on the dot.

While the Scots do have their fair share of American-style 24 hour stores now, those stores still have greatly limited Sunday or holiday hours. And when it's a public holiday, particularly a big one (like New Year's Day), just assume hardly anything will be open at all. We found this out the hard way. On New Year's Eve a few years ago, we arrived at a small coastal village fairly late in the evening, expecting we could eat dinner at a nice restaurant when we got there. We searched all over town, absolutely starving, but nothing was open except a dodgy Chinese takeaway. And my husband *hates* Chinese food. Lesson learned!

The most frustrating part of this is not necessarily the limited hours, but the inconsistency. Some stores might be open, others closed. Or some might open early one day, but not open until later the next. Or the hours posted on the door might say a store should be open, when it isn't. Going shopping requires the expectation of occasional inconvenience.

RETAIL PARKS

Contrary to popular belief, soulless strip malls and shopping complexes are not unique to the United States —

they have invaded Scotland's suburbs as well. Known as retail parks, these complexes are populated mainly by large format chain stores, one of which is typically a supermarket. Sometimes these places make it easy to forget you're not in America, minus the familiar storefronts. And it's just as hard to find a parking spot.

THE TOUN

Pronounced "toon", **the toun** (town) is the nearest major town or city to you. So if you were heading into Glasgow you'd say *"I'm going into the toun."* The **city centre** is the downtown area of the toun. And the city centre is where you'll find the High Street.

THE HIGH STREET

Every town and city has a **High Street**, a shopping district where all the big national chain retailers are found. In Glasgow, Sauchiehall Street and Argyll Street are both considered major High Streets, as is Princes Street in Edinburgh.

A view down Sauchiehall Street in Glasgow.

Walk down any High Street, and you'll usually find any combination of the following shopfronts (with examples):

Mini versions of chain supermarkets	Sainsbury's Local, M&S Simply Food
Cafes	Costa Coffee, Caffè Nero
Bookstores/greeting card shops	WH Smith, Waterstones, Birthdays, Clinton Cards
Chain bakeries	Gregg's
Chain restaurants and eateries	Pizza Express, Bella Italia, Pret a Manger
Chain pubs	Wetherspoon's
Chain opticians	Specsavers
Charity Shops	Oxfam, British Red Cross
Chemists	Boots, Superdrug
High Street fashion retailers	Primark (cheap!), NEXT, River Island, Topshop, Dorothy Perkins, Burton, H&M, Miss Selfridge, Zara, TK Maxx, Mango, New Look
Pound shops (the equivalent of dollar stores)	Poundstretcher, Poundland
Mobile phone shops	O2, Orange, Phones4U
"Mother & Baby" shops	Mothercare, Mamas & Papas, JoJo Maman Bébé

THE WONDER THAT IS TRIANGLE SANDWICHES

You'll never have to wonder what to have for lunch when you're out and about, because wherever you go, you can be confident that there's a triangle sandwich *somewhere* nearby. They are sold everywhere, from bookshops, to chemists (pharmacies), to corner shops, to castle visitor centers. They come in triangular boxes, predictably enough.

You'll be spoiled for choice when it comes to fillings, but some of the old familiar standbys include cheese and onion, prawn mayonnaise, tuna and sweetcorn, chicken and bacon, and egg & cress.

A typical triangle sandwich selection at a small shop.

THE PUB

One of the first things to know when you step into a Scottish pub is that the bartender is either a **barmaid** or a **barman**, as old-fashioned as that sounds.

The *gantry* is the shelves behind the bar where bottles of spirits are displayed. If a place is said to have a great gantry, it has a good selection of spirits (especially whiskies).

A casual pub in the toun.

The food served is affectionately known as *pub grub*, and it's usually stodgy, stick-to-your ribs fare. Pubs don't always serve food, but they will have crisps, nuts and other snacks for your beer munchies.

One thing to take note of: there is normally no table service in pubs. You usually have to go up to the bar to order (this is also sometimes even true in restaurants.) On the plus side — no tipping, remember?

It's standard practice to take turns buying rounds when you drink with friends. Everyone takes a mental note of whose round it is, so don't think people aren't keeping "tabs" on who goes up to the bar next.

At pubs of all types, you'll usually find a *puggy* or two, which is a one-armed bandit or fruit machine. There will also be the usual accessories you'd expect: a dartboard, pool table, snooker, etc. They will have fun nights scheduled, like karaoke or open mic night, or pub quizzes.

It's "Karaoke Night" at the local.

If you frequent enough pubs, you might eventually be part of a *lock-in*. This is when the pub landlord essentially "locks in" his guests after legal drinking hours to be able to continue serving them. During a lock-in, the pub turns into a "private party", and as long as nobody else comes in for drinks during this time, the people in his pub are considered personal guests.

11

get in my belly:
a glossary of grub (and glugs)

"My theory is that all of Scottish cuisine is based on a dare."
- Mike Myers

SCOTS, LIKE us, *love* their food. And in my humble opinion, there's no better way of getting acquainted with a culture than through its food.

"AMERICAN" FOOD

One thing I find amusing is the attempt at "American" food in prepackaged food products. They try, but they never get it *quite* right. You can tell they're trying because they're sure to put lots of stars and stripes on the packaging. In my earliest days of living in Scotland, there was always a can of "American hot dogs" at my mother-in-law's house. Yes, canned hot dogs. You dump the brine out, replace it with boiling water, wait a bit, and voila, hot dogs. Yeah, we don't do that here.

Note: For Americans who have lived in Scotland for considerable amount of time, homesickness sometimes manifests itself as cravings for comfort foods from "home" that are no longer easily accessible. Needless to say, faux American food doesn't quite cut it. Some of the most common cravings: Kraft macaroni and cheese, grape jelly, saltines, real maple syrup, pumpkin pie (or any sweet pie for that matter), pumpkin spice anything, real American-style peanut butter, Mexican food, Graham crackers (and likewise, s'mores), and Triscuits.

BEER

A lot of people like beer, but Scottish people and beer go way back. 5,000 years to be exact. There's evidence of beer brewing in the neolithic settlement of Skara Brae. Look in any pub on any given day, and you'll see guys lined up along the bar with their pints. While women Stateside swig beer right alongside the guys, that's a lot less common in Scotland. (That's not to say you can't enjoy a pint if you're a woman, you're just a lot more likely to be the only one drinking it, in my experience.) When a bottle of beer is served *by the neck*, it is not poured into a glass. But, most people just ask for a pint.

There are several categories of Scottish beer:
- **Wee heavy** - a strong beer or barley wine, served in smaller measures.
- **Export** - can be found on drought at most Scottish pubs, though it was originally brewed for consumers abroad (hence its name)
- **Heavy** - Similar to Export, but slightly weaker and lighter in color.
- **Light** - darker than "Heavy" but less alcoholic

Tennent's lager (brewed in Glasgow) is one of the most popular beers in Scotland, so you'll no doubt see it everywhere, with its unmistakable red T logo. Fun fact: From 1965 until 1991, cans of Tennent's featured pictures of glamorous models, known affectionately as "Lager Lovelies". These cans are highly collectible now.

BRIDIE

A bridie is a savory pastry filled with meat and onions. Fun fact: Bridie is short for "bride's pie" because they were originally served at weddings.

BROWN SAUCE

Similar in flavor to steak sauce, HP brown sauce is as popular as ketchup (also sometimes called red sauce) as a condiment in Scotland. It's usually paired with savory breakfast foods, bacon or sausage sandwiches, or chips. Note: The Scots pronounce it *broon* sauce.

CHEESE

The UK is famous for cheese, and Scotland is no different. For truly Scottish cheeses, there's **crowdie**, a lowfat cream cheese often eaten on oatcakes, and **Dunlop**, which is similar to mild cheddar and pairs well with whisky. Some supermarkets use a cheese strength numbering system where 1 is very mild, and 5 is seriously strong. (The system isn't standardized though, so it varies from store to store.)

CLOOTIE DUMPLING

A vintage dessert that most people outside of Scotland haven't heard of is clootie dumpling, a fruitcake-like pudding cooked in a large cloth bag. (Clootie means cloth in Scots.) Until recently, they were served on children's birthdays with a sixpence cooked inside. I've only seen it on a menu once, at a B&B in Oban. Clootie Dumpling is also supposedly a nickname for the Scottish National Party (SNP).

COCK-A-LEEKIE SOUP

The name says it all. It's a soup made from cocks (yes, that in fact means chicken) and leeks. The original recipe called for prunes, but that probably doesn't appeal to most modern taste buds.

COFFEE

Because tea is the hot drink of choice, most people are perfectly happy keeping a jar of instant at home, so bear this in mind when asking for coffee at someone's house. If you want your coffee with milk, ask for *white coffee*. Note: There is no half-and-half or non-dairy creamer because everyone just uses milk to whiten their tea or coffee. There *is* single cream (heavy cream) and double cream (which, as you can imagine, is doubly as creamy). But again, they only use milk.

If you're someone who likes/needs real, strong coffee and uses a French press like I do, note that they are called *cafetieres*. (I had the hardest time finding one once for this reason.)

CRANACHAN

Cranachan is a very Scottish combination of whisky and oats, sweetened with raspberries, honey and cream.

CRISPS

Scots can't get enough of their crisps (potato chips), and why not? There is a ridiculous variety of unusual flavors to choose from, like roast chicken dinner, Worcester sauce, or tomato ketchup. I've even seen haggis flavored. The most popular crisp flavors are cheese & onion, salt & vinegar, prawn cocktail, or ready salted. Fun fact: they're called "ready salted" because they're *already* salted. Some crisps come *unsalted,* and actually include a separate packet of salt in the bag to shake on yourself!

CULLEN SKINK
Despite the name, cullen skink is actually a highly edible creamy chowder made from smoked haddock (usually the Scottish variety called **finnan haddie**), onion and potato.

FRENCH TOAST
French toast, also called eggy bread, is considered a savory meal, not sweet, and it's often eaten with ketchup. (Blasphemy.)

FULL SCOTTISH BREAKFAST
Nothing starts your day off like a good "fry-up", which usually looks a lot like this:

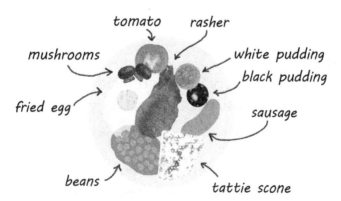

A note about breakfast in Scotland: the way we Americans

mix sweet and savory is considered disgusting. You'll never, for example, find pancakes drenched in syrup on the same plate as your bacon and eggs. (Similarly, we would never in our right minds consider beans a breakfast food.)

JUICE

Diluting juice (also called *squash*) is shelf-stable, highly concentrated fruit juice that you water down to your desired strength. (Somewhat self-explanatory.)

Speaking of juice, while grape may be America's purple fruit of choice, in Scotland it's blackcurrant. (Grape juice, or grape flavored anything, is seriously hard to find.) The most popular brand of blackcurrant juice is Ribena, which most kids grow up drinking by the juicebox-ful. It's marketed as healthy because of its high vitamin C content, but it's loaded with sugar (because blackcurrants are actually ridiculously sour in real life).

Note that lemonade is not what you think it is — it's a clear fizzy soft drink, like 7up, and used as a mixer with beer to make shandy.

Also note that in Glasgow, any carbonated soft drink can be called *juice*, even if there's no juice in it whatsoever. If you're at a bar and want actual orange juice in your drink, you have to specify "fresh orange".

LUCKY BAG

A lucky bag is a mixture of assorted sweets, usually from a *sweety shop*. *Sweeties* in Scotland usually means candy (although it's also slang for drugs in some circles. But we're talking about candy here.) One thing to know about Scots is that they have a serious sweet tooth, so if you do too, you'll find no shortage of opportunities to get your sugar fix. (Irn Bru, anyone?)

A "lucky bag" self-service station

MINCE

Ground meat, most likely beef, is known as mince. Mince and tatties (ground meat and potatoes in gravy) is classic Scottish comfort food.

Fun fact: Mince is also a Glaswegian word for utter nonsense. Mince can also be used to describe someone or a team not performing to the best of their ability. *"Rangers played mince today!"*

OATS

"Oats: a grain which in England is generally given to a horse, but in Scotland it supports the people."
- Samuel Johnson

That was quite the low blow from Samuel. But seriously, since the Middle Ages oats have been a staple crop in Scotland, since so little else grows in such a dreich, sun-starved climate. As a result, oats have always been a mainstay in the traditional Scottish diet (even haggis has some stuffed in there).

What we call oatmeal is called **porridge** in Scotland. And **oatcakes,** which are very strongly associated with Scotland, aren't cakes at all: they're salty, savory crackers.

A classic Scottish oatcake.

PIECE
If someone asks you if you want a piece, don't say "a piece of what?" because in Scotland, a piece means a sandwich. Sausages between two slices of bread is called *piece and sausage,* a jam sandwich is a *piece and jam,* a

salmon sandwich is a *piece and salmon*, and so on and so forth.

PLAIN & PAN LOAF

Scottish plain loaf is a type of white bread made exclusively in Scotland and Ireland. It has a *well-fired* (dark) crust on the top and bottom, but the sides remain crustless (the loaves are baked in batches then torn apart).

Pan loaf is the same as plain loaf, except its crust goes all around the bread. It was once regarded as the fancier variety, so the term "pan-loafy" meant snobby or stuck up.

PLONK

Inexpensive, unpretentious, everyday wine you pick up at the supermarket is affectionately referred to as plonk. Always good to know.

POITIN

Pronounced po-cheen, poitín is pretty much Irish moonshine made from potatoes (of course). Warning: it is ridiculously strong. A hint would be the fact that "póit" means hangover. In *Irish*. It can reach a stratospheric 90% alcohol by volume, which is stronger than absinthe. Even seasoned drinkers can find themselves on the floor, grasping to "hold on" after a shot or two of poitín.

SCOTCH BROTH

Scotch broth is a thick soup made with lamb or beef and root vegetables. You can find a tin of it in many Scottish cupboards.

SCOTCH PANCAKE

A Scotch pancake is similar in size to our silver dollar pancakes and are already sweetened with sugar. They are eaten cold with butter or jam.

SCOTCH PIE

A pie in Scotland is savory, *not sweet*. They are individually sized, like thick hockey pucks. Scotch pies, as they're called, contain minced meat and have a firm crust over the top, which makes them portable. A very traditional dish served in pubs nationwide is "pie and beans". Calling someone a "pie" is also a mild insult.

STOVIES

If you have potatoes and onions, you can make stovies, a thrifty Scottish way to use up leftover meat and/or vegetables. Everything gets fried together in a big pot, creating a dish that's perfect for a chilly day (which is, let's face it, most days in Scotland).

SHORTBREAD

Super rich, sweet and popular too, shortbread (*shortie* for short) has it all. It comes in any shape imaginable, and is strongly associated with the Christmas and New Year season. (Its name comes from the fact you must handle the dough for as short a time as possible.)

TABLET

If your sugar cravings are at critical levels, you'll love tablet, which is literally nothing but sugar, butter, condensed milk, and more sugar. It has the soft texture of fudge, with the added crumbliness of all the glorious sugar that's packed into it.

TEA BISCUITS

What we call cookies are known as biscuits in Scotland, and they are usually paired with tea. Pantry staples are either **digestives** or **rich tea biscuits**, which come stacked in wrapped cylinders, and are not too sweet (unless you go for the milk chocolate topped varieties). There are also **Jaffa Cakes** (a chocolate coated soft cookie with orange filling), **Jammie Dodgers** (jam cookies) or **Hobnobs** (oat cookies usually with milk chocolate), just to name a few. There is also the very Scottish **Tunnock's Teacake**, which is a marshmallow on top of a biscuit covered in chocolate (sort of regarded as a national treasure). A **Tunnock's Snowball** is the pretty much the same thing covered in coconut. Then there is a **Tunnock's Caramel Wafer**, layers of biscuit and caramel covered in chocolate. If you have a sweet tooth, you can't go wrong — all are good.

WHISKY

Whisky is famous worldwide for being Scotland's national drink. That said, I'm actually surprised at how rarely I've seen actual Scottish people drink the stuff straight up. You'd think it would be their go-to tipple, but they're just as likely to drink any other spirit, if they bother with spirits at all. Straight whisky is kind of seen as an old man's drink, and for everyone else it's most likely only consumed on special occasions, when they "break out the good stuff". But when they do, they do it with great enthusiasm. Because it's whisky, and they're Scottish!

Older people might call a glass of whisky a *goldie*. A *dram* means a drink of whisky, rather than a precise measure of it. You might also hear *wee hauf*, which means the same thing. (Note that a hauf could also refer to half a pint of beer, but when you ask someone out for a "wee hauf", significantly more than half a pint is generally involved. As per usual.)

There are two main options when buying whisky: *single malt* or *blended*. Single malt is the product of a single distillery (not necessarily from the same barrel), and blended is a mixture of products from several different distilleries. It's that simple. The final product must mature three years before it can be sold as true Scottish whisky.

Some whiskies are described as *peaty*, meaning they have the smoky flavor that comes from actual peat (decomposed organic plant matter compressed in the ground for thousands of years). Some hate it, and some love it. An Islay whisky, produced on the island of Islay at the southern end of the Outer Hebrides, is among the peatiest flavored of Scottish malts.

Moray/Speyside is where you will find the highest concentration of whisky distilleries in Scotland — Glenlivet, Glenfiddich, Aberlour, and Macallan, to name a few.

Takeaway

Takeaway (what we call takeout) meals are tremendously popular and tend to make up a good portion of the average Scottish diet. It's not unusual to get a takeaway at least once a week. In fact, I'd even say if you want to truly understand the Scots through food, you should start right here.

Most takeaway places are literally designated for takeout — on rare occasions they might have a table or two, but they aren't full restaurants. You can call ahead and pick up, but if you're feeling extra lazy, most of them will deliver straight to your door.

CHIP SHOPS

A chippie in Glasgow, ready for its Saturday night post-pub rush

The most ubiquitous type of takeaway is the chip shop (*chippie* or *chipper* for short), the all-purpose purveyor of deep fried food in all its greasy glory — pure comfort food, with high fat and carb content. Example: a *fritter roll* is a deep fried potato pancake on fluffy white bread. (This is the reason love handles are called *chip hips*.)

Consequently, it's also ideal "drunk food". Downtown on a Friday or Saturday night, they attract drunk people like moths to a flame. You'll see them lined up at these places at 2 or 3 in the morning, which are often conveniently located near bars and nightclubs.

Everything that comes out of a chip shop is encased in thick, golden batter with a generous dusting of salt, usually served up in styrofoam or similar boxes.

Traditionally they serve fish and chips, but anything is fair game. The only vegetable you'll find on the chippie menu is likely onion rings. I've watched my husband in horrified fascination scoffing down deep fried personal pizzas, deep fried burgers, and footlong deep fried sausages. Deep fried haggis is another popular offering.

Thanks to fryer-happy chippies, we also have the infamous *Deep Fried Mars Bar*, one of the many inventions Scotland can take full credit for, right? Basically it's a Mars chocolate bar (Milky Way), deep fried in batter to achieve a golden, crispy coating. It's notorious for being the worst of Scotland's cardiac-arresting eating habits. I have never tried one, and believe it or not, neither have most Scots. (They're for the tourists).

Anything that comes out of a chippie with a side of chips (fries) is known in Scotland as a *supper*. So, pizza and chips is a "pizza supper" and fish and chips is a "fish supper". If you don't want chips, you ask for a *single*. So fish without chips is a "fish single". Note that singles usually include two of an item, so you'd get two sausages in a "sausage single". (Yeah, that doesn't make much sense to me either.) A *poke of chips* is a paper cone or small bag of chips only.

To Scots, a portion of chips is only worth its salt if it's drenched in malt vinegar. In fact, salt and vinegar is one of the most popular crisp flavors too. They really can't seem to get enough of that sexy potato-vinegar flavor combo. Fun fact: malt vinegar is made from ale, just like red wine vinegar is made from real red wine. One thing you'll notice in Edinburgh: when buying a supper from a chip shop, you might instead be offered salt and sauce as a topping. (The sauce is some combination of vinegar and ketchup.)

Typical condiments beyond malt vinegar include gravy, cheese or *curry sauce*. And the mention of curry brings me to my next point...

INDIAN
My personal favorite takeaway is Indian, which was introduced decades ago by the large Indian and Pakistani population. Indian takeaway menus are extensive, with any

imaginable style of curry in varying levels of spiciness, and they even offer a smaller "European Menu" with things like burgers for less adventurous palates. (Many people will also order a side of chips with their Indian food.) And the Indian food in Scotland is good, oh so good. If you're not familiar with it, **Chicken Tikka Masala** is a delicious place to start (it was actually invented at an Indian restaurant in Glasgow!) Don't forget to order garlic naan on the side. The ultimate starters are pakora and samosa, so be sure to try them both.

KEBAB SHOPS

Turkish takeaway places are called kebab shops. They are famous for **doner kebab**, which is meat shaved off a vertical rotisserie. (You'll often see these gigantic rotating slabs of meat through the window as you walk past these places.) The meat is usually stuffed into pita bread with various toppings, which might actually include fresh vegetables — a rare sight in the Scottish fast food world.

THE MUNCHY BOX

A Glasgow invention, the munchy box has now made its way into the hearts of Scottish people all over (specifically, their arteries). It's basically a large pizza box packed full of a 5,000 calorie assortment of whatever fast food your favorite takeaway has to offer. A typical munchy box might include garlic bread, onion rings, deep fried sausages, kebab meat, chicken wings, fried pizza, all on a bed of **Glasgow salad** (otherwise known as chips).

CHINESE

Chinese food in Scotland is not really the same as what we're used to the the US. (Not that "Chinese Food" in

Western countries is authentic anyway.) I never associated spicy curries with Chinese cuisine until I went to Scotland. Nor would I associate chips as a Chinese side dish in lieu of rice. Also, prawn crackers. Lots of prawn crackers.

AMERICAN

Just like anywhere else in the world, there's no shortage of McDonald's, Burger Kings, KFCs, and Pizza Huts in Scotland. Needless to say they aren't going anywhere either, because they are hugely popular.

MEXICAN FOOD, OR LACK THEREOF

There is no real Mexican food in Scotland. And there's just something about not having access to Mexican food that makes Americans who spend any considerable length of time there crave it immensely. (Which is understandable.)

Getting the messages (food shopping)

The messages refers to your routine grocery shopping. It's very confusing to the non-Scottish ear because it basically makes no sense, but you get used to it. When you get home with your shopping bags, you say you're bringing the messages in, and when you're unloading them, you're putting them by.

A Marks & Spencer somewhere in Glasgow.

An interesting phenomenon to take note of: across the UK (not just Scotland), you're a teeny tiny bit judged by where you choose to do your weekly grocery shopping.

Marks & Spencer (or M&S, nickname Marks & Sparks) and Waitrose are the top tier choices, followed by Sainsbury's. Then there's Morrison's, followed by Tesco. ASDA, which is literally Walmart (they are the same company under a different name) comes next. Below that, are frozen food retailers Farmfoods and Iceland. The list bottoms out with Aldi and Lidl, with a reputation for being dirt cheap. (Fun Fact: Trader Joe's and Aldi share the same parent company.) There's a twist, however: with the economic downturn, penny-pinching M&S shoppers have taken a liking to these two German budget supermarket chains, elevating their status and therefore forcing the more expensive shops to drop their prices to compete.

Major supermarkets, for the most part, look pretty much the same inside as American ones — minus any recognizable brands on the shelves. For that reason, you tend to get that "uncanny valley" feeling within a few seconds of walking in the door. Even food that looks like it *could* be familiar often is just that teeny bit different. Take the cereal aisle, for example. Cheerios and Rice Krispies are always sweet, and Frosted Flakes are called Frosties. In Italian food, instead of ricotta, you'll frequently find a bland white sauce known as **bechamel**.

Pizza seems like it should be safe, but look closer and you'll notice freaky toppings, like tuna and sweetcorn, or cheddar. Something as basic as food shopping can easily take three times as long because you have to stop and examine *everything*. Many Americans living in the UK joke that they have experienced "supermarket meltdowns" in their earliest days

Where the actual fuck am I?!

for this reason, brought on by a combination of hunger and confusion. Think of it as a treasure hunt. And don't be afraid to try new things. You might be surprised to discover your new favorite food.

Shopping carts, parked outside in a shelter next to the entrance, are known as **trolleys**. They usually require you to insert a pound coin in order to release one, and the only way to get your money back is to return the trolley. (This supposedly prevents theft.)

Looking around a typical supermarket, you'll notice that there is usually a large portion of the refrigerated section is devoted to "ready meals", pre-made single serving dinners which you cook in the microwave. These meals are sealed with plastic film which you puncture with a fork to cook, similar to our frozen dinners. But they're fresh, not frozen, so they're actually edible, and frequently include fresh vegetables which get perfectly steamed as they cook. You can almost always find good deals on them, and they're pretty perfect for lazy nights when you just can't be bothered to cook.

Moving on to dairy: to make things slightly more confusing than necessary, the lids on milk cartons are the

reverse colors of what we are used to. Whole milk in the US almost always comes with a red top, but in Scotland a red top always means Skimmed. Completely the opposite. In the UK, you can pretty much count on Semi-Skimmed (reduced fat) milk having a green lid, and Whole milk having a blue lid.

Another thing that might startle you is that eggs are sold on shelves, unrefrigerated. And people will store their eggs right on the kitchen countertop. *Unrefrigerated.* The eggs-planation for this is that salmonella is less of a risk in Europe, because chickens are vaccinated against it. Also, unlike the US, British eggs aren't washed, meaning they still have their protective coating (and sometimes feathers and… other stuff too.) Even the most squeamish person I know who follows expiration dates religiously, leaves her eggs *out of the fridge.*

As you further browse around, you might come across a phenomenon unfamiliar to most Americans — empty shelves. This is rarely seen Stateside unless there is an impending disaster, like a blizzard or hurricane warning. This phenomenon usually occurs later in the day or on weekends, and it's not because of panic buying — it simply means they've run out of stock until the next delivery.

When it's time to check out, you'll notice that the cashiers who work the *till* (cash register) are actually sitting down. At my first job as a cashier in the US, I remember never being allowed to sit down my entire shift, even when there were no customers in the store. They don't bag your groceries either— that's your job. Cashiers definitely have it better in Scotland.

A final thing to note: most shops (even non-grocery stores) now require you to pay a few pence for each plastic bag you use. This supposedly encourages you to bring your own reusable bags.

12

weans, bairns, lads & lassies

Bairn is the Scots word for a young child or baby, but in the Glasgow area they say **wean**, pronounced wayne. (The bus I used to take into Glasgow passed a kids' clothing shop called Weans World, an obvious reference to *Wayne's World*.) Wean is a contraction of "wee ane" which means "little one" in Scots. Some people will say "wee yin". The youngest child in a family is called "the wean".

"Weans World"

In Scotland, your mom is your **mum** or **maw**, and your dad is your dad or **da**. (A dad who visits the pub regularly is known as a **pub da**, for reasons unknown.) A Grandpa is a **Granda** and a Grandma is a **Gran**, with a few variations depending on the family, and grandchildren are often called *grandweans*.

When referring to someone in their family, Scots will add *oor* (our) in front of their name. It makes it clear they are talking about someone in the family, not just anyone with that name. For example, my mother-in-law might say *"Oor Lizzie was in today"*, referring to my sister-in-law. It might also be used in a jocular way, such as *"he may be a bastard, but he's oor bastard."* You know you're finally "in" with a Scottish family when you've earned that "Oor" title in front of your name.

I wish I could reveal some insider's knowledge on the days-in and days-out of raising children in Scotland, but as of yet, my two young children have only lived Stateside. I can, however, share what I know from our extended visits with our kids and being around their cousins.

First of all, what I can tell you from personal experience is that if your spouse is Scottish, your children are automatically dual US-UK citizens by birth. (You'll have to apply for proof of this though.) This is a privilege that your child can benefit from their entire lives, because they'll always have two lands to choose from.

When you have a new baby, it's a very common practice for people to give them a small amount of money for luck. Seriously, when you're walking around your village with your newborn in a *buggie* (stroller), your neighbors might actually hand you a few coins.

Nappies are diapers. Nappy sizes are the same as their US counterparts, and they have the familiar brands. And if you're knee-deep in the nappy years, you'll also come to really appreciate something called Sudocrem. It's a thick white paste that's great for diaper rash, and pretty much any other skin condition you could  think of for that matter. (It also smells really good, almost like cinnamon.)

Dummies are pacifiers, short for "dummy tits". The top of a bottle is also called a "tit" in Scotland. When my mother-in-law used to give my kids their bottles, she would actually say, "here's your wee titty", and my husband and I would quietly share a look of amusement. Funnily enough, nipple, the preferred American term, actually sounds *more* sexualized to the Scots, so it all depends on your perspective.

Cribs are called *cots* and stuffed animals are called *cuddly toys*. A child's sad little pout is called a *petted lip*, and temper tantrums are called *paddies*.

To *nurse* a baby or child does not mean to breastfeed. It simply means to cuddle it. So if someone asks you if you'd mind nursing their baby for a few minutes, don't worry — it doesn't mean that they're asking you to lactate.

This might make a few frazzled moms jealous: in many shopping centers, there is a designated child care area called a *creche* (rhymes with fresh), where you can actually *drop your child off* for a few hours *while you shop*. It's not free, but the fact it exists at all would seem like an unspeakable luxury to the average American mom. Scotland absolutely treats mothers as adult humans who still have adult human interests, while the attitude "you chose to have a kid, now lose your identity" seems more familiar in America.

As the mom of young children, I'm no stranger to playgrounds — and I've really been impressed with the ones I've found myself on in Scotland. Playgrounds are called *play parks*, *swing parks* (or *swingies*), or simply just *parks*, and they are designed like child-sized universes with built-in terrain, winding paths, grassy hills with *chutes* (slides), and some very unique play equipment too, like ziplines. Most of our playgrounds here in the US all look like variations on the same building kit, probably due to safety codes. But my favorite thing of all about Scottish play parks? Gates with closing doors. Almost all of them are enclosed by this minor but extremely helpful feature. If you have a toddler who thinks it's funny to bolt at random and unpredictable intervals, you know what I mean. (I'm no stranger to this phenomenon either.)

And finally, childcare. While you can send your child to private *nursery* (daycare or preschool) to suit your schedule like in the States, council-run nursery is free for all Scottish children from the term after they turn three until school age. Sixteen hours a week. A pretty sweet deal for mums who can make this schedule work for them.

Alternately, there are **childminders,** or professionally qualified sitters who look after babies and young children (usually in the person's own home) while the parents are working.

It's all fun and games...

Blooter	To kick something hard and wildly, like a football for example
British bulldogs	Tagging game similar to "Red Rover"
Carry-code	Piggyback ride. (Might also be called *backie, coalie-backie, coal carry,* or *cuddyback.*)
Five-a-sides	Casual game of football with your mates (five players per team)
Keepie-uppie	Juggling a football without letting it fall to the ground, using only the feet, knees, head and chest.
"Keys!" or *"Keezies!"*	Yelled out during a game when you want a truce or a temporary suspension of the rules.
Naughts & crosses	Tic-tac-toe. Naught means zero (for the O's) and crosses refer to crossing out (for the X's).
Tig	Tag

Getting schooled in Scotland

First of all, there are no yellow school buses. (Yellow school buses are one of the more unique things about America.)

At most schools, both private and public, uniforms are required. The argument for them is that while they can be a pricey investment at the beginning of the school year, they end up saving parents lots of time and money in the long run to not have to buy so many clothes. And, since everyone is dressed the same, it supposedly levels the playing field a bit to not have to worry about buying into trends or brand names. (Although, sadly, that does eventually matter too.).

School holidays are the school vacation days children get throughout the year. These days vary by location, but school normally starts in mid-August, and lets out in late June. However, Scottish students seem to get many more days off during the school year than most American students get. Looking at the calendar for my nieces' primary school, there's a long weekend in September called "September Weekend", a few days off again in October, two weeks off for Christmas and New Year, a couple days off in February, two weeks off again in April ("Easter Holidays"), and a few days off again in May.

Primary school is the rough equivalent of elementary school. Instead of grades Kindergarten through 5, the years go from Primary 1 through Primary 7. In America, elementary school starts at age five going on six, whereas in Scotland, Primary starts the year you turn five (so some students will start at age four). Primary 7 is age ten going on eleven.

High school, or *Secondary school*, comes immediately after Primary school. (There is no equivalent of middle school.) Students start High school at age 11. The years are Secondary 1 through Secondary 6, with an option of leaving after S4. Students in the UK are only legally required to go to school until they are sixteen. If you leave school at sixteen, you're called a *school leaver* and it just means you've chosen to join the working world a bit sooner.

If the student plans on attending college or eventually university (they're different things), they will stay in school and concentrate on a couple of subjects relevant to the degree they plan on studying.

UNIVERSITY IN SCOTLAND
As an American who has been to *uni* (university) on both sides of the pond, I would say that the primary difference is that in Scotland, students focus primarily on their subject of interest from the start. You don't take courses in any other subject, so you must know from Day One exactly what you want to study for the next three (or more) years. (No dabbling!)

Depending on the university, there are usually thee terms instead of two semesters. There is also a lot less "contact time" attending classes and lectures. At the same time, a lot more independent research on your own time is expected. Whether you pass or fail weighs very heavily on self-discipline and personal motivation for that reason. Instead of many small tests, there are several big exams usually in essay format (and they tend to be marked strictly). All in all, it's a more serious, academic environment, with less of the perceived chumminess between professors and students that you might expect at an American university.

More School Terms to Know

Canteen Cafeteria

Dogging school Skipping school

Dinner lady Lunch lady

Jotter Exercise book or notebook (any book you write in).

Jannie Janitor. (Apparently jannies are best known for their talent at pouring sawdust over puddles of puke.)

Lollipop lady/man Crossing guard. (The stop sign they hold to direct traffic at crosswalks looks like an oversized lollipop.)

Maths Math

Play piece Packed lunch brought from home (piece means sandwich)

Pritt-stick Brand of glue stick

School dinner School lunch

Tipp-ex Wite-out equivalent

13

things you should know before you go

If you plan on spending any time in Scotland at all, you'll run into all of these things eventually, so you might as well acquaint yourself with them.

TEMPERATURE

The weather forecast is given in degrees Celsius. Thankfully there's an easy trick to convert Celsius to Fahrenheit in your head: double the number and add 30. (So, 10°C would be about 50°F.)

CLOCKING OUT

Scots formally go by the 24 hour clock. It takes some getting used to, but after a while it becomes second nature that 13:00 is 1pm, 14:00 is 2pm, and so forth. But in everyday conversation, the 12 hour clock is used. However, as with many things, I quickly learned that *even telling time* is different:

- While an American would say "five-thirty", a Scottish person would say **half five**. (They prefer to divide their clocks into fractions over there. Quarter past, quarter to, etc.)

- ***The back of an hour*** is the time just after it, up until about twenty past. So, if you were making plans for 7ish, you'd say, *"I'll meet you at the back of seven."*
- ***Yon time*** means an unspecified time very late at night. *"We'll not be hame till yon time at this rate."*
- Speaking of clocks: In Scotland they say ***anticlockwise*** instead of counterclockwise.
- Now is ***the noo***. And ***just now*** means "at the moment". *"I'm busy just now, could you phone me back later?"*
- ***British Summertime*** refers to the timeshift we call Daylight Savings Time, when the clocks "spring ahead" an hour in the springtime. But this time shift happens a week or so *after* ours. This means that, on the U.S. East Coast where I live, the time difference between us and Scotland is very briefly four hours instead of the usual five. The same thing happens in Autumn when clocks "fall back".

THE CALENDAR

- Dates are written DD/MM/YY. (We Americans are the odd ones out in the world with our MM/DD/YY nonsense.) Bear this in mind when checking expiration dates. If it says 12/6 on your yogurt, that's the 12th of June, not December 6th!

- Often calendars will start the week on Monday, not Sunday. Bear this in mind too, because more than once

I've gotten a Scottish calendar from my in-laws for Christmas and have written something on the wrong day without checking.

- Another thing: Scots think it's awkward how we Americans say *"See you Tuesday."* To them, it sounds like we're skipping a word. They'd say *"See you on Tuesday."*
- A *fortnight* is two weeks. (The word is short for "fourteen nights", to help you remember.)
- Tomorrow is *the morra*, as in *"See you the morra!"* (In some parts, tomorrow is *the morn*, and the day after tomorrow is the *morn's morn*.) Today is *the day* and tonight is *the night*. Basically, replace "to" with "the".

MONEY

A British pound sterling (GBP), the basic unit of currency in the UK, is represented by the pound sign (£). There are 100 pence (p) in a pound. The coins are 1p, 2p, 5p, 10p, 20p, 50p, £1, £2.

Banknotes (bills) in the UK are in denominations of £5, £10, £20, and £50, just like ours. Scotland prints its own unique set of banknotes that say "Bank of Scotland" on them, featuring Scottish imagery and notable Scots.

But even though English banknotes are readily accepted everywhere in Scotland, the reverse is *not true*, which is frustrating because Scottish money is perfectly legal tender throughout the UK. (There are no unique Scottish coins, however.)

This Scottish twenty pound note is legal tender everywhere in the UK. (Don't let anyone tell you otherwise!)
Coins, left to right: £2, £1, 50p, 20p. 10p, 5p, 2p, 1p

Quid is the slang word for pounds, like bucks is for dollars. But quid is never plural. It's always just quid. Something that's £50 is fifty quid. Nobody says bill either, it's always either **note** or **banknote**. A **fiver** is five pound note. A **tenner** is a ten pound note.

Two bob, which is 10 pence, can also mean a small amount of money. If someone's short on cash, you'd say *"they don't have two bob to rub together."*

...And if you don't have any money at all, you're **skint**.

POSTCODES

Postcodes are like zip codes, but a postcode includes both numbers *and* letters, and it also gets you within a few houses of any given address.

PHONE NUMBERS

Unlike the US, the area code can be anywhere from two to five digits, and always starts with zero. The area code for Glasgow is 0141, Edinburgh is 0131, and Dundee is 01382, for example. When you call a UK number from the US, first dial the country code (011 44) and always drop the initial zero in the phone number. When you call the US from the UK, add (001) then area code, etc.

TO YOUR HEALTH

When it comes to healthcare, the state-run Scottish NHS (National Health Service) means it costs little to nothing for doctor visits, dental care, prescriptions, surgery or X-rays. In other words, Scots will never face debt or bankruptcy from medical bills, because healthcare is free at the point of use (already paid for by taxes).

When you're not feeling well and you look a bit pale and under the weather, you're *peely-wally*. But you're not sick, you're *ill*, unless you're actually vomiting. (Sick means puke or the act of puking.) You might then head to the *chemist* (pharmacy) for some *paracetamol* (the exact same thing as Tylenol). If you have a cold, you might go for *Lemsip*, a lemon-flavored powder which you pour boiling water over to make into a soothing hot drink.

If you get a cut or scrape, you put a *plaster* (Band-aid) on it, but if you break a bone it's time for a *stookie* (cast).

Assuming you're a woman, if you're due for your period, you might have a touch of **PMT** (Premenstrual Tension, what we call PMS). Then you might say *"the painters are in"*, which means Aunt Flo is here for her monthly visit.

A Scottish anatomy lesson

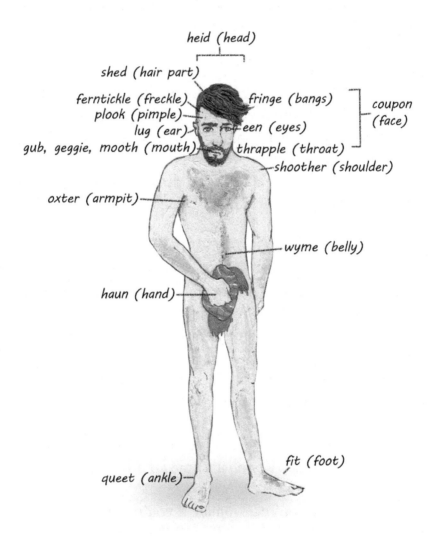

heid (head)

shed (hair part)

ferntickle (freckle)
plook (pimple)
lug (ear)
gub, geggie, mooth (mouth)

fringe (bangs)

een (eyes)

thrapple (throat)

coupon (face)

shoother (shoulder)

oxter (armpit)

wyme (belly)

haun (hand)

fit (foot)

queet (ankle)

WEIGHTY MATTERS

When you're asked your weight in the UK, people don't expect you to state the actual number on the scale. Your weight is measured in *stone*, which is equal to 14 lbs. Because 14 lbs. is such a ridiculously wide range, you usually round up or down to the nearest half stone. If you're 143 lbs, you'd say you're 10 stone. (And no, it's never plural. Always just stone.)

SIZING YOURSELF UP

Women's clothes are sized like this (although, as always, it varies from retailer to retailer):

6-8 is X-Small,
8-10 is Small,
10-12 is Medium,
12-14 is Large
14-16 is XL ... and so forth.

To get a rough idea of your shoe size, subtract two and a half from your American size if you're a woman. So if you're a US 9, you can assume you're about UK 7.5. For men, just subtract half a size. So a US 11 would be a UK 10.5.

Never just assume your size. Clothes and shoes tend to be more expensive, and return policies are not nearly as lenient as they are in the States. I would actually advise to do all your clothes shopping Stateside if possible. (There's a reason people go to the US for "shopping holidays".)

Getting dressed: your claes

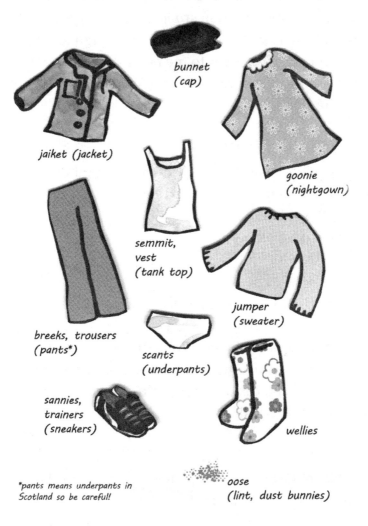

jaiket (jacket)

bunnet
(cap)

goonie
(nightgown)

semmit,
vest
(tank top)

jumper
(sweater)

breeks, trousers
(pants*)

scants
(underpants)

sannies,
trainers
(sneakers)

wellies

*pants means underpants in
Scotland so be careful!

oose
(lint, dust bunnies)

14

cultural references: a crash course

OBVIOUSLY, THIS is *far* from an exhaustive list. But if you want a sweeping idea of what's on the radar of Scotland's national consciousness, it's not a bad place to start.

ALEX FERGUSON - Scottish football player, now better known as the legendary manager of Manchester United (England).

ANDY MURRAY - A Scot famous for being the most successful tennis player of all time from the United Kingdom. He is also famous for being called "British" when he wins, but "Scottish" when he loses.

BALAMORY - Popular kids' TV show based in an imaginary location in Scotland.

BIG ISSUE - A magazine sold by homeless people on the streets to give them a legitimate source of income.

BRAVEHEART (FILM) - The 1995 film starring a Mel Gibson which most people think of when they think "Scottish history". It's based on the story of William Wallace, who led the war for Scottish Independence 600 years ago. Scots love the film. When you hear Scottish people shouting "FREEEEDOOOOOM!" they're ironically quoting the most famous line out of Braveheart.

BURNISTOUN - A sketch comedy show starring Iain Connell and Robert Florence. Recurring characters include Biscuity Boyle whose trousers are always falling down, and Doberman Man (a superhero who is haunted by the fact he is still a virgin).

CHEWIN' THE FAT - A sketch comedy featuring popular Scottish comedians, most of whom who went onto star in the spinoff show Still Game, which became far more popular. (See **Still Game**).

FRANKIE BOYLE - Comedian famous for his very un-PC dark humor

GERARD BUTLER - An actor who is generally regarded as a Scottish heartthrob.

JACKIE BIRD - Newsreader/presenter who is famous for hosting Hogmanay programming on the BBC

JEELEY PIECE SONG - A Scottish children's folk song that happens to feature a ton of Scots words. The chorus goes:
Oh ye cannae fling pieces oot a twenty story flat
Seven hundred hungry weans will testify to that
If it's butter, cheese or jeely, if the bread is plain or pan
The odds against it reaching us is ninety-nine to wan.

KRANKIES - An unintentionally disturbing cabaret act starring a married comedy duo. What makes it disturbing is that the wife plays a schoolboy (Wee Jimmy Krankie) and the husband plays "his" dad (Ian Krankie). They coined the catchphrase "fandabbydozy", which means great. Their popularity peaked in the 1970s and early 1980s, but the mental scars won't soon be forgotten.

KEVIN BRIDGES - A young Glaswegian comedian who does observational humor on the Scottish way of life

LIMMY - A lowly Glaswegian web developer who accidentally rose to fame in the 2000s because of his personal website that featured an interactive swearing xylophone, among other "playthings". He eventually got his own surreal comedy show on the BBC.

OUTLANDER - A currently popular time-travelling drama set in Scotland.

RAB C. NESBITT - A comedy series starring an unemployed, unwashed alcoholic slob from the Govan area of Glasgow and the unbelievable messes he gets himself into with his loser friends and family. (You'll most definitely need subtitles for this one.)

RIVER CITY - A long-running Scottish soap opera based in the Glasgow area (hence the name River City, after the River Clyde).

RICKY BURNS - Scotland's most successful boxer. Scotland has many boxers, but he's one of the best.

SCOTCH & WRY - A sketch comedy featuring legendary Glasgow comedian Ricky Fulton. Popular sketches included "The Reverend I.M. Jolly", and "Supercop" — whose catchphrase was *"Alright, Stirling, oot the car."*

STEAMIE, THE - A beloved stage play set entirely in a Glasgow steamie (wash house) in the 1950s. It offers a glimpse into the lives of a group of women who, back then, spent a great deal of their lives slaving away in steamies (before the invention of washing machines). The 1988 TV version of the play is broadcast every year on Hogmanay.

STILL GAME - A TV series starring two lifelong pals (Jack and Victor), now widowers and pensioners, who live in a high rise tower block in the fictional town of Craiglang. Together with their friends and associates, they get into all sorts of hilarious jams.

SUPERGRAN - A popular 1980s kids TV show featuring a Scottish grandmother with superpowers battling against her nemesis, Scunner Campbell.

SEAN CONNERY - Oscar-winning Scottish actor best known for playing James Bond and his intereshting pronun-she-ationsh of wordsh.

SKINNY MALINKY LONG LEGS - an old children's schoolyard song.

> *Skinny Malinky Long legs, big banana feet*
> *Went to the pictures, and fell through the seat.*
> *When the picture started, Skinny Malinky farted*
> *Skinny Malinky Long legs, big banana feet.*

SUSAN BOYLE - A frumpy, middle-aged Scottish singer with a strikingly beautiful voice who rose to international fame after appearing on Britain's Got Talent.

TAGGART - A Glasgow-based crime series from the 1980s originally featuring Detective Chief Inspector Jim Taggart, played by Mark McManus (until he died in 1994).

TRAINSPOTTING (FILM) - A very popular, extremely dark 1996 film starring Ewan McGregor, featuring a gang of junkies and lowlifes in the Edinburgh area and the tragic (and sometimes humorous) situations they get into. Recently, a sequel has been made with the original cast set 20 years on from the original (Trainspotting 2).
Note: "trainspotting" is the exceptionally nerdy hobby of going to train stations and taking note of the numbers on the trains that pass.

THE BIG YIN - Otherwise known as Billy Connolly, one of the most famous Scottish comedians ever.

WEIR'S WAY - Basically, a show featuring an old man (Tom Weir) who stoats through the Highlands showing you out-of-the-way places in Scotland while saying *"isn't this beautiful?"*

WICKERMAN, THE - A cult 1970s B-movie horror about a devout Christian encountering Godless pagans on an isolated Scottish island. Spoiler alert: he is eventually sacrificed inside a giant burning man made of wicker. The (recently defunct) annual Wickerman Festival in Kirkcudbright was inspired by this film, climaxing with the burning of a giant 30 foot wicker man at midnight in the middle of a field. (I've been to two of these.)

YE CANNAE SHOVE YER GRANNY AFF A BUS - A song of unknown origins, sung to the tune of "She'll Be Comin' Round the Mountain":

Ye cannae shove yer granny aff a bus,
Oh ye cannae shove yer granny aff a bus,
Ye cannae shove yer granny, for she's yer mammy's mammy,
Ye cannae shove yer granny aff a bus.

Ye can shove yer other granny aff a bus,
Ye can shove yer other granny aff a bus.
You can shove yer other granny, for she's yer daddy's mammy,
Ye can shove yer other granny aff a bus.

15

things scottish people (actually) say

THERE ARE A lot of Scottish dictionaries out there, but I've compiled a list of the words and phrases I've actually heard people say most often in real life (and that didn't really fit anywhere else in this book). You'll probably hear them frequently as well, particularly if you find yourself in the Glasgow area (roughly a quarter of all Scots live within twenty miles of Central Glasgow, so you'll more than likely encounter most of these yourself too.)

AGES WITH
If you're the same age as someone else, you're "ages with" them.
"Fiona is ages with her cousin, Callum."

ASKING FOR
Americans say: *"Tell your mom I said hi."*
Scots say: *"Tell your mum I'm asking for her."*

AT IT
At it means up to no good or being dishonest.
"He took another day off work. He's at it."

BASTARDIN'
Bastardin' is used the same way bloody or damned is.
"That bastardin' fly keeps gettin' away from me!"

BRAND NEW
When a person is described as brand new, they are an all-around good person.

BIRL
To birl means to spin.
"My heid is birlin'!"

BONNIE
Bonnie means easy on the eyes. Even though it's easily one of the most Scottish of Scottish words ever, nobody really uses it much anymore. And the first name Bonnie? Not really heard much in Scotland. It's more common in America.

BUBBLE
To bubble is to sob noisily.

BRIG
Brig is the Scots word for bridge. If a place has "bridge" in its name, it will often get shortened to "brig" too. For example, the town of Coatbridge is sometimes called Coatbrig by locals.

BREW, THE
When you're "on the brew", that means you're unemployed and receiving unemployment benefits.

CLAP

To clap means to pat an animal.

CHAP

To chap a door means to knock it.

"I chapped the door earlier, but naebody answered."

CRACKER

When something's referred to as a cracker (or *smasher*), it's really great. It's often used to compliment friends' babies.

"He's a wee cracker."

DADDY LONGLEGS

In America, daddy longlegs are those weird spidery things. In Scotland, daddy longlegs are craneflies, long-legged beasties that are always getting into the house.

DINGHY

To dinghy someone means to ignore them or give them the cold shoulder. (Another term for this is *rubber-ear*).

"I dinghied him yesterday."

DODGY

Dodgy means untrustworthy, or of questionable legality. It can refer to places, things, or even people. The Barrowlands marketplace in Glasgow hits all three of these marks, giving it its well-earned reputation for dodginess. You can also say you have a dodgy tummy if you're having GI issues.

DOOFER

A doofer is another word for the TV remote.

"Ah cannae find the doofer."

DUG
A dug is a dog.
*"I **clapped** my dug when she brought me ma slippers."*

DUNT
A dunt is a thump or blow to the body. It can also mean feeling the effects of, say, alcohol.
"Have you got a good dunt off thae pints yet?"

EASY-OASY
Someone who is easygoing and laidback is easy-oasy. In America, we'd call them "chill".

EMPTY, AN
When you're a teenager and your parents are away and you have the house to yourself, you tell your friends you have an empty. (In other words, it's party time.)

FAIR DOOZE
Fair dooze is said to acknowledge someone's witty observation or retort. Kind of like "fair play" or "touche".

FOR AGES
For ages is the most common way to say a very long time.
"We've been waiting at this taxi rank for ages, but have not seen a single taxi."

GALLUS
When someone is gallus, that means they're bold, daring and somewhat reckless. (In Glasgow, it's a compliment.)

GIE IT LALDY
This means give it all you've got.

GREET
When a Scot is greetin', they ain't welcoming anyone.
They're crying like a baby. A good greet is a good cry.
Someone who is always miserable and complaining about
everything will be told to "quit yer greetin'."

GROG
To grog is Glaswegian for what we would call hocking a
loogie. It also means the product from such an action.

HAVER
To haver is to blab about nonsense.
"And if I haver, I'm going to be the one havering to you."- a line
from the famous Proclaimers song, *I'm Gonna Be (500 miles)*.

HEEHAW
Heehaw means absolutely nothing.
"I got heehaw in my bank account."

HINGMY
Hingmy is a word used when you can't think of the name of
something, similar to how Americans say "thingamabob" or
"whatchamacallit".

HOACHIN'
Hoachin' means really badly overcrowded, or swarming
with something. A pub can be hoachin' with people, a
campsite can be hoachin' with midges, or a burger can be
hoachin' with grease.

HOLE

To *get one's hole* means to have sexual intercourse. (Both men and women will say it.)

HUNNERS

Hunners means any number over, say 5. (Hunners = hundreds.)

I'M AWAY TO...

When you say you're away somewhere, that means you're heading there any moment.
"I'm away to the shops. Do yous need anything?"
"Right. Half eleven. That's me away to my bed."

IN THE SCUD

In the scud means naked.

J

The letter J is often pronounced "jie" (rhymes with pie). So when you hear someone say the alphabet, it sounds like "H, I, Jie, K..."

JAGGY

Jaggy means prickly. A shot at the doctor's office is also referred to as a jag. (It's also a nickname for a stinging nettle.)

JAKIE

A jakie is an alcoholic, usually a down-and-out.

JAMMY

Jammy means ridiculously lucky. (You can also say *spawney*.)

"You jammy bastard!"

JOBBY

Jobby is a word for excrement or rubbish. Synonyms include **shite** or **keech**.

KEEN

If you're keen on something, you like it. Likewise, if you're not keen on something, you don't like it.

"I'm not keen on that 1970s wallpaper."

KEN

In some parts of Scotland, ken means know. Oftentimes people will end a sentence with *"ye ken?"* which means "you know?"

KNOCK ONE'S PAN IN

When you've knocked your pan in, that means you've worn yourself out from hard work.

LEATHER, TO

As a verb, to leather means to give someone a beating.

LONG LIE

When you're having a long lie, it means you're sleeping in. On New Year's Day, nearly everyone in the country has a long lie.

MA BIT

Ma bit means my house. Yer bit means your house.
"Come over to ma bit."

-MERCHANT

Adding -merchant to the end of any word refers to a person who is very fond of that thing or activity. For example, a bevvy-merchant is someone who loves to get drunk.

MIND

To mind something means to remember it.
*"Mind when we used to go to Jim's **bit** for Hogmanay?"*
"I cannae mind the last time we went."

NAE DANGER

Nae danger means no worries.

NINETEEN-CANTEEN

Nineteen-canteen means some undetermined year in the past, a long time ago.
"He's worn that same stripey jumper since nineteen-canteen."

OCH AYE THE NOO

Och aye the noo means….. just kidding, nobody says this. Somewhere, somehow, someone decided that it's something Scottish people say *all the time*. Although the phrases "Och aye" and "the noo" are used all the time separately, they are rarely used together like this phrase suggests.

OFFSKI

When you say "I'm offski", you're announcing your hasty departure.

ON YOUR KITE

When you've went on your kite, that means you've slipped or tripped and fallen.

"That ground is icy. Nearly went on my kite there."

ON YOUR TOD

When you're on your tod, that means you're on your own.

"I went to the pictures last night on my tod."

QUERY

The word query is often used in place of "question".

"Any queries can be directed to Gillian in accounting."

PURE

A very Glaswegian way of saying totally.

"That's pure class!"

"The club was pure hoachin', man."

"The bus drove past me and I was pure ragin'."

PISH

Pish is a multipurpose word that can mean either urine or to urinate, the state of being drunk (pished), or utter rubbish.

"Wit a load of pish!"

PUIR WEE SOUL

When someone or something, like a puppy, is endearing in a pitiful way, you might say *"ah, the puir wee soul"*, which translates to "poor little thing".

RIFT
A rift is a burp, or the act of burping.

SCOOSH
Scoosh means easy.
"That exam was a scoosh."

SCOOBY
Scooby is rhyming slang for clue. (Scooby Doo = Clue.)
When you haven't got a scooby, you haven't got a clue.
"I haven't got a scooby where my other sock went."

SCREW THE NUT
To screw the nut means to get your act together.
"I finally screwed the nut and joined the gym."

SCUNNERED
When you're scunnered, you're sick of something.
"It's been raining for three weeks and it's scunnered me."

SKELF
A skelf is a splinter, or something that gets under your skin.
It can also be used for a tiny, skinny person. (My
mother-in-law once said I was a wee skelf when I first
moved to Scotland, and I'm still not entirely sure which one
she meant. Still love her though.)

SKELP
A skelp is a slap or smack.
"Yer gettin' skelped if ye don't mind me."

SHOOGLY
Shoogly means shaky or unstable.

SIDEYWAYS
Sideyways is how Scottish people say sideways.

SMOUT
A wee smout is a child or undersized adult.

SNOUT
A snout is a slang term for a cigarette.

SOAPY BUBBLE
Soapy bubble, or just soapy, is Glasgow rhyming slang for trouble.

SOUND
Also used in Liverpool, England, sound is a highly complimentary way to describe someone you like a lot, even though it's often paired with cunt. (Gotta love those Scots.) *"He's a sound cunt."*

STOATER
A stoater is anyone or anything fantastic or exceptional in quality, from a well-played goal in football, to an attractive woman. But adjust the tone ever so slightly, and stoater can just as easily become an insult. *"He's a pure stoater."*

STAY
Where you stay is where you live.
"I stay down the road just past the lochs."

SWATCH
A swatch is a look at something.

THAT'S YER _____ DEID
If someone you knew but were not particularly close to has died, like a neighbor in your village, someone might announce it to you like this.
"That's yer Auld Rab deid."
(Deid is pronounced deed.)

THAT'S YOU/THAT'S ME
When you're finished with something, you can simply say *"that's me."* It can also start a sentence.
"That's me finished my work for the day. See yous later."
Alternately, *"that's you"* is used to tell someone "you're all set".
"Right, that's you, all ready for school."

TAKE A TELLIN'
To take a tellin' is to be mindful of a warning or a scolding.
"I warned ye, but ye wouldn't take a tellin'."

TEA'S OOT, YOUR
When someone says *"your tea's oot"*, they haven't made you a hot drink. It signals that you are about to get into a fight/challenge.

TOTIE
Totie means very small. The word comes from "tot", as in small child (which was originally a Scottish word).
"She's just a totie wee thing."

TAKE A FLAKIE
To take a flakie means to have a temper tantrum. (Can apply to both children and adults alike.)

WEE
Wee means little. Anyone who knows anything about Scotland knows this. And yes, Scottish people say it. All the time.

XX
XX is a double kiss. Scottish people don't actually *say* this, but they write it after their name in greeting cards, at the end of text messages, etc. Some people, women especially, use it compulsively as a sign-off in just about every written interaction.

(Note: We Americans are guilty of doing the same thing, but we use exclamation points!! instead.)

YOUS
Yous is you, plural. It's the equivalent of saying "you guys" or "you all". (It's a damned useful word, don't yous think?) *"See yous later!"*

ZED
Just like the rest of the UK, the letter Z is said "zed", not "zee".
"Phew, finally reached the end of this book and Ah'm pure scunnered. Ah'm away tae ma scratcher tae catch some zeds."

Made in United States
Orlando, FL
25 February 2023